Starting
Fieldwork

Starting Fieldwork

Methods and Experiences

Judith E. Marti

WAVELAND

PRESS, INC.

Long Grove, Illinois

For information about this book, contact:
Waveland Press, Inc.
4180 IL Route 83, Suite 101
Long Grove, IL 60047-9580
(847) 634-0081
info@waveland.com
www.waveland.com

Contents

PART 1
Going into the Field:
Things You Need to Know that Are Often Hidden

PART 2
Methods

Contents

About the Author

Dr. Judith Marti was Emerita Professor at the California State University, Northridge, where she taught from 1982 until her retirement in 2012, teaching classes on gender, economics, and field methodology, and mentoring countless graduate students. She graduated suma cum laude from the City College of New York with a dual BA in History and Anthropology, and received a PhD in Anthropology from UCLA. She was the Secretary Treasurer of the Society for Economic Anthropology from 1996 to 2009. Before becoming an anthropologist, Judith was a professional photographer and a medical lab technician. She has traveled extensively throughout Latin America, Europe, and the Middle East, where she lived with the Jordanian Bedouins in the 1960s (depicted below). Her professional research interests encompassed economics, gender, labor, and immigration in the US. This is her second book with Waveland Press.

Foreword

In 2010, my mother, Dr. Judith E. Marti, was working on a historical anthropology text for Waveland Press's series of teaching modules on special topics in the discipline. After discussion with Tom Curtin, her Waveland editor and good friend since the early '90s, she felt there was a lack of guidance for young anthropologists starting fieldwork and decided to create a small, accessible book on methods—the book you are now reading. Although Russell Bernard's comprehensive guide was—and still is—an excellent resource, Judith saw the need for a smaller work specifically tailored to beginners, one that could serve as both a resource for classroom teaching and an independent guide for the novice fieldworker. Unfortunately, Judith passed away on August 25, 2015, while in the process of doing the final stylistic edits.

This book was very important to Judith on many levels. A professor at California State University, Northridge, she taught the anthropological methods course for many years, guiding students through their first fieldwork experiences in multiethnic Los Angeles neighborhoods, as well as supervising her own graduate students in their research locally and abroad. She has always considered mentorship to be very important; in addition to her own students she mentored numerous younger faculty and colleagues, and has worked with outreach programs for high school students and the public.

Speaking as an anthropologist, I am glad to see this resource being made available to benefit future fieldworkers. But, speaking as her daughter, I can say that writing this book also benefitted Judith herself. Working on the book gave her personal strength and fulfillment through a very difficult stage of her life. In 2013 she was diagnosed with lung cancer, and through two years of medical hardships she continued to make progress on this manuscript: writing and reading, exchanging emails and phone conversations with anthropologists, photographers, and museum curators. Thus she continued to do what she did best, and to be what she was at her very core: a researcher and a mentor to others. When she passed away, she had completed the full manuscript and was in the process of doing the final edits. She had also accumulated notes for her next book, on visual anthropology and documentary photography.

We are very pleased that Judith's work has reached the publication stage so she can continue to mentor future students. The final stylistic edits were completed by myself and Oscar Marti (my father and Judith's husband of 47 years). We added this foreword to the final manuscript and submitted it to Waveland as she intended. The book, however, is very much hers. We hope it will aid future researchers for years to come.

F. Alethea Marti
Center for Health Services and Society
University of California, Los Angeles

Preface

FOR THE STUDENT

This book is for you, the budding anthropologist, who is about to do fieldwork across the globe or right at home. Armed with course work and readings in anthropology, you suddenly find yourself in the field for the first time, which can be daunting. This book, it is hoped, will not only serve as an introduction to the methodologies that are in the anthropologist's toolkit but, equally important, give you assurance through examples from seasoned anthropologists and students. Learning what to expect, being exposed to possible solutions, and just knowing you are not alone are tremendous assets to take to the field.

You will have questions. What if nothing happens in the field? What if no one talks to me? What if I don't get any data? No one really knows what is going to happen in the field, but the reality is that *something* will happen. Here you will learn how to be flexible and handle new situations, and that it's OK to change your mind when your research takes you in a different direction than planned. And you will learn how your life experiences can enhance your understanding, how serendipity plays a role, and how you yourself will be changed.

Here is one student's experience:

> I was initially hesitant to drive all the way to Artesia [Little India] by myself, somewhere I had never been, and then when I got to this unfamiliar place, seek out strangers to talk to and

try to get to know. That was definitely daunting for me, considering I tend to keep to myself around people I am not familiar with. Then, I felt there was an extra layer of nervousness because I kept thinking "What if they don't speak English?" "What if they hate me?" "What if I do something disrespectful that I have no idea what I'm doing?" The list goes on of all my self-doubts but considering that the assignments were set up almost like baby steps it definitely was nice to my nerves. That way I could build up confidence slowly and make significant progress that I could track. However, I pushed through my fears and conquered each assignment with a sense of adventure. . . . I was definitely surprised at how emotionally attached I became to my ethnic enclave and the people that I talked to there. During my last trip there, after I had finished doing my fieldwork, I felt very sad as I walked to my car.

If you are doing fieldwork for a class, then it will be close to home. You will discover that learning to recognize the usual can be more of a challenge than studying the unusual—our surroundings are so familiar to us that they become invisible. Gerry Tierney stressed "the importance of understanding what is going on in your own backyard before thinking about going off to exotic places" (Tierney 2007: 10). And according to the American Anthropological Association, today more anthropologists will take jobs close to home outside of academia, in nonprofit associations, government agencies, world organizations, and corporations. The experiences you acquire in doing fieldwork for a class and the feedback from your instructor will train you for these roles.

The students in my methodology classes live in a large urban city—one of the most diverse in the United States. Each student chose as a field site areas of the city with immigrant populations. Some selected an ethnic enclave (Little Tokyo, Chinatown, Koreatown, Little India, Little Armenia, Cambodia Town, Thai Town, and more). Other students wanted to work with populations that were more scattered, such as Irish or French, or enclaves that were more hidden, such as Croatian. Students made many forays to their field site during the semester. But you don't have to live in a large city to study immigrants. There are immigrant populations in almost every part of the country, in towns big and small and in rural villages.

FOR THE INSTRUCTOR

This book has two goals. The first is to provide the instructor a compact, concise introduction to anthropological methodology that can be used in the classroom for upper division undergraduate students as a companion to other texts, ethnographies, or materials. Even given its small size, the book covers the basics found in larger books on the subject, but it also fills several important gaps. It covers participant-observation, considered the backbone of methodology, but adds areas not always covered, such as museums and archives as field sites, the camera as methodology, and photographs as evidence. Though there are several good books on writing field notes, this book focuses on the jottings that precede that step. And it brings the topic up to date by looking at digital anthropology and autoethnography. Finally, it has sought particularly to present what is often hidden and to consider what others have said to be unteachable.

The second goal is to let students know what they can expect in the field, especially when things go wrong (which they will), and how others have handled these situations. It lets them know that feelings of isolation, loneliness, and anxiety are felt by everyone in the field and how others have overcome these feelings. Going into the field, even when equipped with the best training, is daunting. Students need to know that they are not alone, that this is a normal part of fieldwork. These topics are touched on in some books and articles but they are often scattered. From blogs, interviews, and other readings I have pulled them together in one place. Students will hear the voices of well-established anthropologists and of other students like themselves. These lessons need to be given equal weight with traditional methods in anthropology.

This short, accessible introduction to methodologies and life in the field is filled with real life experiences to which instructors can add their own voice. The instructor will have his/her own opinions on many aspects of fieldwork. This book allows for that. Here you will find questions rather than answers. It is not a book of rules, but rather guidelines that consider many approaches and allow for discussion.

Acknowledgments

I want to acknowledge with gratitude the many people who helped and encouraged me to work on this book: To my colleagues at CSUN, especially Suzanne Scheld, Christina von Mayrhauser, and Stephen Siemens, for their comments and suggestions; to Akiko Arita, Matthew Halpern, Holly Haverty Woolson, John Pulskamp, and the many students who took my course and from whom I learned so, so much; to my many good friends at the SEA, Katherine Browne, the late Rhoda Halperin, Lynn Milgram, Josie Smart, Tamar Wilson, Martha Woodson Rees, and others too numerous to remember from my failing memory.

I want to thank my editor, Tom Curtin, whose guidance and advice were always on the mark, and whose encouragement and patience were priceless; to my doctor, Gary Schwartz, for having given me life enough to finish the book; to Michelle Patos, my research assistant; to my precious children—my son, Edward, for the intelligent feedback and encouragement, and my loving daughter and best friend, Alethea, for everything.

And finally, I want to thank my husband, my love, companion, soulmate, and source of strength in sickness and in health. . . . To him I dedicate this book.

Sherman Oaks
August 7, 2015

PART 1

GOING INTO THE FIELD
THINGS YOU NEED TO KNOW THAT ARE OFTEN HIDDEN

Chapter One

Breaking Anthropologists' Taboos

Anthropologists study taboos in other cultures, but we are reluctant to look at our own taboos. Among anthropologists there is a taboo not to discuss certain aspects of fieldwork. This is unfortunate because it can be a roadblock to doing anthropological fieldwork: You have to know what to expect when you go into the field.

One exception to this taboo occurs during the wee hours of the morning when anthropologists gather to relax and unwind. Here is how it happened to me: It was midnight, the last night of the American Anthropological Association (AAA) annual meeting, and the hotel bar was full. Clusters of anthropologists were gathered around small tables drinking and doing what anthropologists do best—telling stories. These bar stories are striking in how much they differ from the formal presentations that have been going on all during the previous week. They are stories from the field. First come the one-upmanship stories—the poisonous snakes in my field site were deadlier, I was sicker (certainly near death), it was colder (hotter, rainier, swampier) than anyone else's experiences. Then, as the evening turns into morning, stories became more personal—involving loneliness, feelings of isolation, anxieties, not being understood, and shear boredom. Finally talk turns to a real taboo among anthropology academics that is seldom published: about fieldwork stalled and failed, when one is faced with the impossibility of carrying out a research plan—the necessity of changing a topic or field site or just abandoning the project altogether. Blame is first placed on bureaucratic red tape or the inability to get people to talk. But finally there is the fear that it might be one's own fault, that one might just be unprepared, not well trained, or that "maybe I'm just not good enough."

These discussions in the bar serve an important function at the conference. Sometimes solutions are offered that solve an ongoing problem or prove useful at a future date. But more important is the support they give. As I listened, the stories brought back memories of my own first fieldwork experiences while pursuing my dissertation. In that bar I felt a flood of gratefulness to those who were so courageous and honest about their experiences and a wonderful feeling, "I am not alone." These were experienced fieldworkers, whose work I greatly admired, and they were recounting similar feelings to those I had experienced in my first forays into fieldwork as a graduate student. I wished someone had imparted them to me before I left for the field. A purpose of this book is to do just that. Learning what to expect, being exposed to possible solutions, and just knowing you are not alone are tremendous assets to take to the field.

Margaret Mead tells us that when she was studying, young researchers were sent into the field with little or no warnings of what to expect. She writes, somewhat facetiously, "and if young fieldworkers do not give up in despair, go mad, ruin their health, or die, they do, after a fashion become anthropologists. . . . But it is a wasteful system" (Mead 1993 [1972]: 74).

Things have begun to change. Here and there you can find published accounts of what one will face in the field, and graduate students today are blogging for each other about their experiences and feelings in the field. But these lessons need to be given equal weight with traditional methods in anthropology and made accessible in one convenient place. Fieldwork is the backbone of the anthropological endeavor. Ethnographies are the final products of years of fieldwork. But what appears on the printed page often makes it appear that doing fieldwork is seamless. Bianca Williams (2011:28) writes, "While some are becoming more honest about this, it still may not be mentioned during fieldwork methods courses. It is the one thing frequently hidden in those fantastic narratives included in published ethnographies." Often missing are the day-to-day fieldwork experiences that make up that data collection—both positive and negative. We are left asking what is it like to do fieldwork? How does it feel in the field? What should we expect? What should we know? What should we do? Anthropology students are sent out equipped with method and theory, but less so with the skills and knowledge needed to navigate the often choppy waters they will find there. Here you will be introduced to ways to navigate.

WHAT THEY DON'T TELL YOU

You Are Not Alone

Bianca Williams writes about her dissertation research:

> I remember entering my field, now what? That feeling of not knowing what to do, where to go, who to talk to and who to trust, haunted me for days. While I vaguely remembered reading ethnographies where the authors *briefly* mentioned these obstacles, it seemed impossible that they experienced the same confusion and aimlessness I was experiencing. I mean, their stories always ended with an argument tied up in a pretty bow, right? (2011: 28)

She forced herself to go out and meet people but "this feeling that I wasn't doing fieldwork or research right resulted in weeks of anxiety and self-doubt. There was a brief period when I gave up, reading books and watching an endless loop of dance hall videos in my apartment, only leaving to walk to the grocery store." She finally called two professors who readily admitted they, too, had experienced such feelings in the field—more than once and "not just at the beginning" (28). Once she discovered that she was not the only one—that what she was experiencing was common—she was able to begin work. She gives this advice: "Give yourself some room to breathe and adjust to your field site. Allow time for the unforeseen, and know that what you are going through is part of the fieldwork experience and your research" (2011: 28).

Amy Pollard (2009) expressed similar thoughts. She and her fellow PhD students often faced challenges that their prefieldwork training had hardly prepared them for, including "a range of feelings: alone, ashamed, bereaved, betrayed, depressed, desperate, disappointed, disturbed, embarrassed, fearful, frustrated, guilty, harassed, homeless, paranoid, regretful, silenced, stressed, trapped, uncomfortable, unprepared, unsupported, and unwell" (Pollard 2009: 1). Was it just bad luck? Was it due to bad judgment? Did anyone else feel as they did? Pollard set out to do a small study interviewing PhD students to find some answers. She found that she was not alone. Negative feelings can come even when fieldwork is progressing. Bronislaw Malinowski wrote of idleness in his diary during a period of time when he was actually at his most prolific (cited in Mead: 1993 [1972]: 74).

Why, I wondered, the first time I was privy to this rite, are students so rarely given these insights? Why is it not part of the curriculum? Could it be because in a highly competitive field to admit failure could be seen as detrimental to one's career? Whatever the reason, I determined then to include these discussions in any methodology class I would teach in the future—and to give students the opportunity to share fieldwork experiences and work through their feelings before venturing out into more advanced research settings. Novice anthropologists should not be derailed due to lack of this training.

This book draws on the work of others who have shared their feelings and experiences, even if unintentionally. As mentioned above, Malinowski kept a diary. It was never intended for publication (Sanjek 1990b: 202). Published posthumously by his second wife in 1967, it was brutally honest and has caused a great deal of controversy ever since. Franz Boas's letters and diaries have been published, but the editor notes: "The sources do not give any indication whether Boas ever considered publishing his personal notes" (Muller-Wille 1998: 5). More recently, anthropologists have shared their feelings in the field on blog sites and in notes in *Anthropology News* (the AAA's newsletter), and some have even incorporated the emotions of doing fieldwork in their ethnographies (see, for example, Anderson 2000; Barley 2000[1983]; Beyer 2007). Graduate student Williams writes in *Anthropology News*, "It is okay to admit you feel alone. . . . I honestly felt like it was a fieldwork crime to admit loneliness to anyone. Somehow I thought that braving the isolation was part of the job and that I had to suffer it in silence." She notes that these feelings (and other things) are not taught in courses or written in many ethnographies—they are invisible. But they are, nonetheless, typical of the fieldwork experience (Williams 2011: 28).

What if Nothing Happens in the Field?

Coupled with the feeling of aloneness is the nagging fear that nothing will happen in the field, that is, nothing worthy of being written up in an ethnographic book or a finished dissertation. Rehenuma Asmi sums it up when she writes: "Would anyone talk to me? Where should I begin? What if I gathered no data? What if no doors opened or serendipity occurred?" (2011: 33). It is good to remember that no one really knows what is going to happen. You enter the field with a project in mind and, if you are fortunate, with funding that resulted from a research proposal outlining that project. But the reality is that anything can happen. If, after a reasonable length of time, the original project really does turn out not to yield results, then you can move on. It is OK to change your mind.

It's OK to Change Your Mind

You may discover, when you begin fieldwork, there are more important questions to ask, different questions that take you in a different direction. Stephen Siemens did his dissertation fieldwork in an Azande village in southern Sudan not far from where E. E. Evans-Pritchard had conducted his studies 50 years earlier (Siemens 1993). In fact, Siemens met several adult men, now elders, who were young children when Evans-Pritchard worked in their village. Evans-Pritchard had written widely about the magic rituals among the Azande—rituals conducted by men—but he did not consider what women did as important or worthy of study. So it was with some surprise that Siemens discovered the importance of women's rituals that mark the beginning and ending of life. He had not intended to focus on women; indeed, he had not been aware of the important ritual roles they took on. But when he did become aware, he changed focus and soon into his research "the 'women's view' moved to center stage" (9).

What if I Don't Like My Field Site?

The Internet has become a venue for discussing taboos in anthropology. Anthropologists have begun to post their experiences on websites such as *Savage Minds: Notes and Queries in Anthropology,* which has become a meeting ground for comments and discussions, opening up an area long closed in the academy. Laura Miller, an anthropology professor, posted the following on that website: "What if we don't like our fieldwork site? I'm not only talking about 'failed research' or the problems of doing fieldwork . . . [of feeling] lonely, fearful, frustrated, depressed, trapped, and paranoid. I have in mind an additional issue: I don't like this place. . . . Why is it a taboo topic for anthropologists to discuss?" (2012).

Miller's fieldwork was successful, and she liked the Russians she met and especially enjoyed their "wicked sense of humor." It was the place she disliked, "the actual physical location—the food, the smell of the air, the toilets, and the other mechanics of being there." Usually in fieldwork situations, once the initial suspicion on both sides is replaced by trust, leaving can be sorrowful and returning something to look forward to. Miller writes that she "never wanted to go back [to Russia] a third time, or ever again." But when it came to her research in Japan, she could not wait to return (2012).

What can account for our reactions to living in another culture? Why do some field sites fill us with joy, while others may bring opposite emotions? Often it is difficult to pinpoint the reasons, even upon reflection after leaving the field. In 1944, Kenneth Read, a trained anthropologist and military man, entered Tofmora village in the Upper Markham Valley in New Guinea on an anthropological assignment for the Australian army. It was wartime and he had few provisions. "When I ran out of food, I existed for three months on whatever the villagers were willing to give me, for by then there was no money to buy the things I needed. Yet this was one of the happiest periods of my life." He speaks of the lovely setting but also describes the lack of privacy and squalid living conditions. The former was not enough to explain his joy, nor did the latter mar his feelings. The lack of privacy made this a difficult adjustment for one who, he admits, is by nature introverted, but "I was as much at ease with some of them as I have been with only a few other people" (1965: 7). He found he sought out others for the sheer pleasure of their company. Several years later he returned to New Guinea, this time to work with a tribal people, the Gahuku. He was welcomed in Gahuku, unlike Tofmora where many wanted him to leave the next day, but never felt happy in this village. Although there was a lack of privacy in both villages, in Gahuku he felt "smothered" (1965: 23). His feelings of "inner exhaustion and mental protest" (1965: 22) were something he lived with on a daily basis and eventually led to a stomach ulcer that required his swift removal to an army clinic.

TAKING THE FAMILY TO THE FIELD— IT CAN BE A BOON

Anthropologists do not always venture out alone. Many enter the field with family in tow; often it is the anthropologist mother accompanied by children and nonanthropologist husband. Young female anthropology graduate students used to be discouraged from having children until they returned from the field. But based on my own experiences and those of many of my colleagues, I tell my students the decision is really theirs and there are advantages to going into the field with children. A great advantage to having a child of breastfeeding age is it eliminates the worry of contaminated water!

Asmi brought her daughter to the Middle East where she was conducting her dissertation research. She tells us she "was accepted more readily because of my family status and the presence of my daughter," and that "in Qatar . . . children were considered a blessing rather than a nuisance. . . . Having my first daughter with me during my first stint in the field got me invited into the homes of key informants. She was also a wonderful ice-breaker." Asmi also discovered that "being a parent made me a better fieldworker, more aware of the similarly multi-faceted realities of my informants" (Asmi 2011: 33).

In Mexico I found the same to be true. I entered the field with a six-year-old daughter and nine-month-old son. Having children immediately elevated my status—to that of a mother. In the smaller towns, when I started to enter a bus with two children, a folding stroller, and large canvas bag, multiple hands would immediately reach out to take all my burdens. The first time this happened I scrambled onto the bus to find each child sitting happily on a lap and my bag and stroller next to an empty seat waiting for me. Like Asmi, my children gave me an entrée. In the markets, women vendors often brought their small children to the stalls where they would play with toys or produce for sale. When I took my son to the market with me, he was warmly welcomed, and so was I.

When we arrived in Mexico, our housekeeper was scandalized that I had a six-year-old girl who could not handle a sewing needle and promptly set about correcting the situation. She taught her to knit, crochet, and do needlepoint, and these skills further opened doors for me. Women on buses praised her ability and initiated discussions with me, her mother. Little did they know that I could not sew a stitch!

BEFORE YOU BEGIN:
A NOTE ON INFORMED CONSENT

One of the requirements of most university research involving human subjects is institutional approval that the research plan is ethical. Each university has its own Institutional Review Board (IRB) that scrutinizes the research proposals submitted by faculty and students and gives them permission to proceed with the project. Before you begin to write a proposal it is advisable to talk to someone on the board for advice. I have found them to be extremely helpful on the dos and don'ts of the proposal writing. Because cultural anthropology research is conducted in natural settings and does not usually identify the individuals it studies, the research may sometimes be exempt from a full IRB review. But even if your proposal is exempt from the process it may have to get the official stamp of exemption from the board, especially if you are receiving research funding. Each university has its own guidelines and rules.

One aspect of research about humans is informed consent. Informed consent is designed to respect and protect the individual. It informs the subjects studied about the fact that they are being studied and about the risks and benefits, and allows them to choose when, if, and to what degree they want to participate. So that the subjects understand what their participation entails, the consent form should be clear, straightforward, and easy to read. They need to know that it is not a contract, that it is completely voluntary and that they can withdraw at any time, and that there are no repercussions if they decide to say no initially or at any time thereafter. The consent form will be part of your IRB application, and your university's IRB can give you guidelines for how to write one.

There will be times when written consent is not possible, for example if the subject is illiterate. In this case oral consent could suffice. According to the American Anthropological Association website, "informed consent does not necessarily imply or require a particular written or signed form. It is the quality of the consent— not the format—that is relevant."

Consent is an ongoing process in the field. Even though you have made it clear you are "writing a book," and the community members know what your project is about, after a time when you have established rapport, this knowledge is not at the fore. When you are sharing a beer, does your companion remember that what you see and hear might become incorporated in that book? And that you are still, on some level, an ethnographer? The researcher needs to assess the situation and to occasionally remind people about the project.

Chapter Two

Studying at Home
What You Don't Expect

Traditionally, anthropologists packed up their gear and set off to study the "natives" in their natural habitat. A glance at books published in the 1920s and 1930s by well-regarded anthropologists shows this trend: young Samoan girls on the island of Ta'u in the South Pacific (Mead 1928); in Latin America, the Mexican village of Tepoztlán (Redfield 1930); the Azande of today's South Sudan in Africa (Evans-Pritchard 1937). Most studies of the time that were conducted in the United States and Canada focused on American Indians. For example, science fiction writer Ursula Le Guin recounted summers spent in the family summer home in Napa Valley as a small child, where her father, anthropologist Alfred Kroeber, worked collaboratively with her "Indian Uncles," Papago Juan Dolores and Yurok Robert Spott (Le Guin 2004). But even as early as the 1930s, anthropologists began to show the relevance of anthropology to modern Western or urban cultures.

In 1928, Franz Boas published *Anthropology and Modern Life* (Boas 1928). His view was that applying anthropological methods to the study of Western peoples and cultures could show how individuals are shaped by their social environment and offer solutions to current social problems in European and American societies, such as criminality, nationalism, and racism. Boas also used anthropological methods to combat racism by showing that races are culturally constructed concepts, and providing evidence that culture, not biology, is the primary factor in shaping differences in human behavior.

11

Margaret Mead's daughter, Mary Catherine Bateson, writes that William Morrow, head of the publishing company that would publish Mead's first book in 1928, *Coming of Age in Samoa,* asked Mead to add a chapter that would make the book relevant for American readers (Bateson 2001). In 1942, Mead again turned her attention to American cultural traits, this time with the aim of instilling the troops with an attitude that could defeat our World War II enemies (Mead 1962 [1942]).

Hortense Powdermaker is a good example of the shift from studying the "other" in faraway places to working in our own backyard. Her first book, within the tradition of anthropologists going abroad, studied the Lesu of Papua New Guinea (1933). She went on to look at the deep South (1939) and Hollywood (1950).

Today many anthropologists are studying subcultures at home. "What has changed in the last thirty or so years is the relative *amount* of fieldwork in urban and First-World settings" (Jackson 2016: 20). As Russell Bernard and Clarence Gravlee wrote in the preface to the second edition of *Handbook of Methods in Cultural Anthropology,* "Anthropologists today are as likely to be studying urban street gangs or organic farmers as they are to be studying isolated communities" (2014: 12–13).

THE VALUE OF STUDYING AT HOME

Anthropologists studying at home have penetrated worlds hidden, like the high-end world of art collectors (Plattner 1998), and people forgotten, like the victims of Hurricane Katrina (Browne 2015). In 1987, Marvin Harris wrote a book studying modern American life entitled *Why Nothing Works.* Across the United States, from lobster fishermen in Maine (Acheson 1988) to unions in Chicago (Durrenberger and Reichart 2012; Pulskamp 2006), from the daily lives of working-class residents of East End Cincinnati (Halperin 1998) to the daily lives of dual-income middle-class Los Angeles families (Ochs and Kremer-Sadlik 2013), and online communities (Boellstorff 2008; Halpern 2013; Nardi 2010; Newon 2011), anthropologists are studying what makes America tick.

Another area where anthropologists are making their mark at home is their work with immigrant populations. Immigrants can be found in almost every region of the United States, from the largest urban center to the smallest farming community. Their presence in large cities is well-known—Chinatowns in Los Angeles, San Francisco, and New York are tourist destinations. But small towns in the Midwest have also seen large influxes (Leitner 2012). According to the US Committee for Refugees and Immigrants (USCRI), the largest populations of Mon from Myanmar in the United States live in Akron, Ohio, and Fort Wayne, Indiana (see www.refugees.org). Kurds from Iraq have moved to Fargo-Moorhead, North Dakota, and the Hmong from Laos to St Paul, Minnesota. A large percentage of immigrants from India moved to the small town of Millbourne, Pennsylvania ("Online Document: North Dakota Is Absorbing Kurdish Refugees" 1996).

One important reason for studying our diverse population is the trend in anthropology for anthropologists to work outside the academy. According to the American Anthropological Association website, "Since 1985, over half of all new PhDs in anthropology have taken nonacademic positions in research institutes, nonprofit associations, government agencies, world organizations, and corporations" where there is an increasing demand for their expertise, training, and skills. Thus there is the need for anthropologists to study groups in the United States that they will be working with in their careers. And studying populations at home is not only beneficial for those anthropologists who plan on concentrating their studies at home, it is a valuable methodology for any anthropologist, no matter where they plan on focusing their research.

ANTHROPOLOGY AT HOME

Going to an "exotic" place, one expects to find closed doors and is prepared to try to gently pry them open, to unravel the unfamiliar. Studying at home, however, does not mean that things will necessarily be easier. "Fieldwork 'at home' is surprisingly difficult," writes Carol Greenhouse. Americans at work in the US, whose experience and training was researching abroad, "must become anthropologists all over again" (Greenhouse 1985:261). Whereas a foreign culture may seem exotic and has to be made familiar, the opposite is true when studying one's own culture. One has to learn to recognize what is so familiar as to become invisible. Rosaldo calls this "defamiliarization," so that "they will appear—as in fact they are—humanly made, and not given in nature" (Rosaldo 1993: 39).

The Problem of Access

Just because one's field site is close by does not mean it's accessible, that the doors will open easily. For instance, in a study of

Hollywood, Sherry Ortner (2010) cited access as her major problem: Hollywood is a closed community, she said, suspicious of outsiders. She quotes John Gregory Dunne, "What makes accurate books about the machinery of the movie business so rare is the difficulty of obtaining access. . . . What [movie people] cannot control they do not trust, and a reporter with access they view as others might a terrorist" (quoted in Ortner 2010: 211). Ortner further points out that John Caldwell, in a recent book on the movie-making culture, relied heavily on technicians and crew and not on producers and executives, and that in the dissertation written by Ortner's student Alexandra David—*Risky Business: Aspiring Hollywood Actors and the Selling of the Self*—David relied heavily on data collected from actors, on interviews, and on observations (at auditions, acting classes, TV and film sets). Access to the powerful heads of studios, where decisions are made, was off limits (David 2009).

When the Familiar Isn't

Then there is the expectation of familiarity. But one can be *too* close. One thing that prompted Hortense Powdermaker to study Hollywood was that she was a writer and felt a kinship to writers—and therein lay a problem: She could not step outside the role. Rather than seek to understand the role of the writer in the culture of Hollywood's major film studios, Powdermaker was judgmental and wrote of writers "selling out" for large salaries and other perks. Her own value system got in the way, something that she was completely unaware of at the time. Later she would write of this experience: "Conscious involvements are not a handicap for the social scientist. Unconscious ones are always dangerous" (1950: 229).

You can also be too far removed. Barbara Anderson did fieldwork at a United States military base. Because the base was on American soil and peopled with American personnel she expected a common realm of experience. Instead, she found she had entered "a world in many ways as foreign as anything I'd known" (2000: 111). She had entered a world with a whole new symbolic system based on rank and a power structure that had to be learned—from dress codes to salutes and language. The place may seem familiar, she says, but you will be looking at it very differently.

One of my students chose to study Irish immigrants and headed off to a local Irish bar. She was familiar with the Los Angeles bar scene, popular with college students. How different could this bar scene be? There were Irish at the bar, as she had expected. What she experienced was not. "Upon first arriving to the pub I did not expect what would happen when I first stepped foot into the unfamiliar. . . . Everyone there (before I arrived) knew each other and the look of confusion in their faces . . . was that of 'who the heck is that girl, and why is she here? Is she lost?'" Only after several visits did she begin to feel tolerated. The turning point when she was truly accepted, however, came later and will be discussed in chapter 4.

Chapter Three

How Should I Act
in the Field?

Before sallying forth into the field to practice the methodologies outlined in this book, let's talk about the fieldwork experience itself. What should you expect? How will you perceive those you are studying and how will those you are studying perceive you? How will you feel about those you are studying? How will you feel about yourself? What should you know about fieldwork that will make your experience not only less daunting but an exciting, rewarding, and successful endeavor?

HELPFUL TIPS

Be Humble

It was my first anthropology graduate class. I still remember the important lesson that Professor Ronald Himes instilled in us that semester, while weaving tales from his fieldwork in the 1960s in the Tagalog area of the Philippines. "You may be among tribal members," he said, "who have little in the way of material goods, who may live in thatched huts, and who can neither read nor write. But you will soon discover that at least one person, and more likely many members of the tribe, are a lot smarter than you are. Be humble."

Laura Bohannan (writing under the pseudonym Elenore Smith Bowen) in her novel *Return to Laughter* (1964), based on her

17

fieldwork experiences among the Tiv in Africa, recalls her own experience in humility. During a language lesson, leaves were brought out for her to learn to identify. This was not trivial information. Plants meant survival, and children were taught how to distinguish between edible, poisonous, and medicinal plants from an early age. "These people are farmers," writes Bowen, "to them plants are as important and familiar as people. . . . I'd never been on a farm" (16). Although one small boy could name them all, Bowen could not remember even one. The chief, Kako, "gave me that long and incredulous glare with which a brilliant father regards his backward child" (16). Finally the task was given over to Kako's senior wife who took up the role of teacher but with no discernible improvement on Bowen's part: "She set me to learning the same batch of plants; each time I got them miserably mixed" (32).

Today, while many anthropologists have shifted their field sites close to home, this does not mean we understand all that is going on under our own noses. The lesson in humility still holds. Tierney chose to do fieldwork in a homeless shelter in her hometown of Anchorage, Alaska. She writes: "A certain degree of humility is required. . . . It is not, after all, easy to be in the position of one who appears to be constantly in the dark about even the simplest situations." She might have had more book learning than those who lived on the street, but the homeless thought university types were "not very bright about survival on the streets. My willingness to be humble made me a much more acceptable presence" (2007: 13).

Be Patient

Patience is a virtue. Western-trained anthropologists want to plunge in, get things done, and not waste time. These cultural traits cannot be assumed to be universal. I learned that patience can facilitate the research. I am a historical anthropologist, and archives are my field sites. I had been advised to hire a research assistant to help me navigate the rich archives of Guadalajara, Mexico. I was told to find someone who knew the collections and, most important, who knew the archive staff. Angela was that gem. Like myself, she was a graduate student and she had worked for several years in the archives as an undergraduate. I was excited and nervous the first day she brought me to the archive. I was also anxious to get to work. Angela began the day in the archive by greeting every member of the staff, embracing each and asking after the welfare of all the members of their families. One young staff member pulled from her bag a large stack of photos taken on her honeymoon, and for another hour both women oohed over each picture. Then it was time for lunch. By afternoon I was frustrated and angry.

Finally, the young honeymooner asked about my research project. I had barely outlined my main topic—19th-century markets and street vendors—when it was time to leave. I felt I had accomplished nothing and here was my assistant cheerfully saying goodbye to everyone. The next morning, in the same unhappy mood, I rode with my assistant to the archive. This time, after brief greetings, we were escorted to the table that would be ours for the duration of the research. On the table in front of my chair was a stack of documents—all pertinent to my research. This would become a daily routine: brief discussions with my research assistant and a staff member who would produce the next stack of documents. It was only later that I realized what had taken place on that first day. Angela had been doing important work indeed, laying the groundwork for my research by reestablishing her networks in the archive among the staff whose knowledge of the collections was crucial for my work. Thank goodness I had not voiced my frustration (and ignorance) out loud. Patience paid off.

Be Courageous

At the same time that we are eager to start, we are also reticent, fearful, and want to pull back. It takes courage to go into the field, even if the field is one's own backyard. When entering a new field site, the anthropologist should expect to experience feelings of isolation, even in a crowd, while simultaneously becoming the object of study. Feelings of isolation, trepidation, and even panic are not unique to first-time fieldworkers. Students need to know this. Everyone entering a field site for the first time has to start over, making sense of a new culture. Even the most seasoned fieldworker starts afresh, is a novice with every new field site, and experiences these feelings, as I discovered while listening to anthropologists' stories in that bar at the anthropology meetings mentioned earlier. There are many accounts of well-known anthropologists telling us of their initial feelings in the field, how they overcame them, and how things improved.

Malinowski, in *Argonauts of the Western Pacific,* recounts his feelings the first day he set foot on his field site.

> Imagine yourself suddenly set down surrounded by all your gear, alone on a tropical beach close to a native village, while the launch or dinghy which brought you sails away out of sight. . . . Imagine further that you are a beginner, without previous experience. . . . This exactly describes my first initia-

tion into field work on the south coast of New Guinea. I well
remember the long visits I paid to the villages during the first
weeks; the feeling of hopelessness and despair after many
obstinate but futile attempts had entirely failed to bring me
into real touch with the natives, or supply me with any material. I had periods of despondency, when I buried myself in the
reading of novels, as a man might take to drink in a fit of tropical depression and boredom. (2013 [1922]: 4)

But Malinowski persevered: "The first visit leaves you with a hope-
ful feeling that when you return alone, things will be easier. Such
was my hope at least" (2013 [1922]: 4). And they did. Malinowski
wrote, "if you are alone in a village . . . you go for a solitary walk for
an hour or so, return again and then quite naturally seek out the
natives' society, this time as a relief from loneliness, just as you
would any other companionship" (2013 [1922]: 7). Fieldwork was
successful. Malinowski went on to write over 10 books and become
one of the most highly-regarded anthropologists of the century.

Powdermaker describes her first night alone among the Lesu
in Papua New Guinea. "That evening as I ate my dinner, I felt
low. . . . I saw myself at the edge of the world, and *alone*. . . . I was
not scared of the people, but I had a feeling of panic. Why was I
here, I asked myself repeatedly" (1966: 53). "While I was immersed
in gloom visitors arrived . . . bearing a baked taro as welcome." As
they were leaving, they told Powdermaker to "sing out" at any time
for anything. "I was no longer alone" (1966: 58–59).

The first step is the hardest. Powdermaker writes of her Rho-
desia fieldwork: "It still took courage for me to begin interviewing. I
always suffer a kind of stage fright even after many field trips. It
was easy to busy myself doing other things, and I had to force
myself to the first interview." She writes that the first interview "got
me started" and it became increasingly easier after that (1966: 265).

You don't have to go abroad to feel isolated or unsure of yourself. On Tierney's first day in the homeless shelter in Anchorage:
"I . . . felt depressed and wondered what I could have been thinking
of to put myself in this awkward position . . . I had some doubts
about my ability to carry out the project." She tried to make sense
of what she was observing but "you are constantly in the dark
about the simplest situations . . . it can be tedious . . . exhausting"
(Tierney 2007: 13). Eventually, Tierney developed relationships
and began to see how this world, so different from her own, also
was familiar in unexpected ways.

As time passes, things *do* get better, but it is good to remember that all will not be smooth sailing. There will always be frus-

trations, and at times things will seem to be going backward rather than marching ahead. "The 'field' is always a bumpy terrain. In the field one learns to delight in the small successes, roll with the frustrations and never keep score" (Anderson 2000: 177).

My student who spent time in an Irish bar as part of her fieldwork among Irish immigrants describes how surprised, and then daunted, she was when, initially, she was ignored. But she persisted and writes: "I admit that if I didn't get my guts up and go talk to people I don't think that I would have gotten what I did out of that first night."

Be Respectful

"Relax and put your feet up." This is a common Western expression meant to put someone at their ease and make her/him feel welcome. To emphasize the point, one might sink onto the sofa and put one's feet up on an ottoman or coffee table. In some cultures, this well-meant invitation would bring a horrified response. In some Arab cultures, showing the soles of one's shoes is considered a grave insult. What about touching someone on the head? This may be acceptable in some places: In Mexico old women we passed on the street would often rub the top of my toddler's head (his hair was light brown) for good luck. In parts of Asia this would be unacceptable. Gestures we take for granted vary from place to place—how long to clasp a hand in handshake or how close to stand next to a stranger. The same is true for how you address someone. In the Philippines, Michelle Patos (personal communication 2015) says one calls someone older than oneself *kuya* (masculine) or *ate* (feminine) before the first name for someone familiar. If addressing a stranger on the street, just *kuya* or *ate* will do. To not do this is considered very disrespectful. Being respectful is essential, but how does one know what is considered rude or worse in another culture? Finding out is at the top of the list of things to do before leaving for the field. When in the field, watch carefully and do as others do.

SEX IN THE FIELD

Another hidden aspect of life in the field is the subject of sex. Sex and sexual practices have long held a major place in anthropological studies. Early studies include Malinowski's 1929 *The Sexual Life of Savages* and Mead's 1928 book, *Coming of Age in*

Samoa. What has, until recently, rarely been a focus is sex between anthropologists and natives in the field. In a review of the literature, DeWalt and DeWalt note the silence on this subject—both in published books and methodological training in the classroom. They quote Esther Newton on its absence in graduate training. Is it because "interest between field worker and informant didn't exist; would be inappropriate; or couldn't be mentioned?" (DeWalt and DeWalt 2011: 102–103).

Fran Markowitz and Michael Ashkenazi (1999) wrote that, in the 1980s, anthropologists began to focus on what had previously been hidden, such as anthropology's "silent complicity with colonialism" (4). But the question of sex in the field, they note, still remained unexamined. In 1993, after witnessing the distress from a sexual field experience suffered by a graduate student that was "agonizing, self-blaming," the authors thought it was unethical not to address the subject. After they published their book, several more appeared, but the field is still thin. As Don Kulick and Margaret Willson, editors of *Taboo: Sex, Identity and Erotic Subjectivity in Anthropological Fieldwork,* discovered, although many anthropologists "enjoy gossiping about sex, few were willing to write about their own experiences" (1995: ix). But they faced more obstacles than just the reticence of potential contributors. In the preface to their book, Kulick and Willson speak of how their call for papers in the Cooperative Column of the *Anthropology Newsletter* (now known as *Anthropology News*) was initially blocked because the newsletter editors feared such a book would lead to criminal acts.

It is certainly true that anthropologists have crossed the boundaries and found love in the field. Some have formed permanent unions. This should come as no surprise when one spends a year or two participating on a daily basis with members of a community.

But what is the result when the line between lovers, collaborators, and friends becomes blurred? The most important ethical consideration is how this liaison impacts the person whose community you are studying. What are the consequences for the native lover, or for members of the community at large? The consequences of sexual activity are important to consider. Long-term relationships do take place, but in most cases the anthropologist will be leaving the field, alone.

There are also questions concerning research. Will sex in the field enhance an understanding of culture or cloud the research? Can it change how you are perceived for the better because it can lead to acceptance? Or for the worse because you are perceived as a threat? Arguments have been given for and against.

Pros

Some have argued that intimacy can lead to acceptance by the culture and greater insights into cultural behavior and beliefs. Contributors in Kulick and Willson's book talk about how sexuality in the field enhanced their research. They speak of the intimacy that bridges the divide between anthropologist and subject. "Anthropologists, by allowing themselves to be seduced in the field, gain greater ethnographic knowledge and produce more readable and living texts" (Willson 1995: 191). Jean Gearing found that when she became the girlfriend of her collaborator, it increased her acceptance in the community (they later married) (cited in DeWalt and DeWalt 2011: 104).

Cons

But does a single experience of intimacy mirror the norm and bring insight into general behavior? And what of the information gained during intimacy? Can it ethically be used? Another consideration is when there is an existing power difference that changes due to a sexual relationship. Crossing the divide between collaborator and lover can bring unexpected problems that threaten to derail the research. Jill Dubisch was a trained anthropologist studying in Greece. Even as a woman, she gave the orders to her male assistant—until they became lovers. Then she discovered she was expected to take on the traditional role of the female in Greek culture, subservient and obeying. This affected not only her relationship with her assistant but how she was perceived by all the members of the community. Males whom she was able to work with as an equal now perceived her as a subordinate (Dubisch 1995). And what of subsequent researchers entering the field? It may be assumed they are available and open to sexual affairs or seen as a threat based on the behavior of prior anthropologists.

THE PRACTICAL: A NOTE ON SAFETY

As we have seen, initial forays into the field can make one feel uncomfortable, scrutinized, and even unwelcome. As also mentioned, most often these initial feelings will pass. With some effort, people will respond positively, and when you return to your field site, you will be made to feel welcome.

It is important, however, to be able to distinguish between initial feelings of discomfort that arise from feeling unwelcome and feelings of uneasiness because there is the potential of real danger. Are you being scrutinized or are these looks of hostility? In the latter situations you may need to depart quickly. Best, of course, is to not get into these situations in the first place. Avoid areas you know to be unsafe—find out which parts of town are dangerous at night, or even during the day. Parks, unless they are theme parks, are often best not visited at night. Be aware of your surroundings. Watch for warning signs. If you are at all uncertain, leave.

Anderson (2000) had always wanted to visit Thailand, and at the last minute she scheduled a stopover on her way to the Soviet Union. This was not a research focus for her, and she had almost no knowledge of the region. When she asked the British passport officials about going "into the hills" where there were native villages, she was told that this would not be possible, not under any circumstances, but certainly not alone. But back at her hotel, the hotel manager quickly made arrangements for her trip, which should have been a warning sign: "in retrospect, [it was arranged] too quickly" (60). Later, in the remote village where she found herself, there were other hints: It was necessary to lock the doors to safeguard valuables and the expensive silver jewelry worn by women, this in a supposedly poor rural village of farmers, and she was never allowed out of her "guide's" sight. But it was not until she viewed the "corn" fields where, she was told, the villagers worked during the day, and she saw not corn but poppies growing, that the full realization hit. She was in the "Golden Triangle," the largest opium poppy-growing region at that time. Luckily, she made it back to her hotel in the city where at dinner she viewed amazement on the faces of American officers when she related where she had been. They, however, were closemouthed to all her questions.

You don't need to go halfway around the world to experience potential danger. A student related an incident in class as a warning to other students. He visited a park during the day where old men played chess and mothers brought their toddlers to play. There was a soccer field and a basketball court. It looked safe and felt safe—until he returned at night. The day visitors had left, and it was not until he was some distance into the park that he became aware of a group of young men approaching him from across the soccer field. He could not be sure of their intentions and looked around nervously. Fortunately, coming from the opposite direction he saw a young priest from the church across the street from the park. The priest caught up with him, and recognizing the young men, spoke with them as well. Then he suggested to my student that he accompany him to the street and bus stop. "I know these boys," said the priest. "I work with them. They are gang members, but probably would have done you no harm. Nonetheless, it is best that you stay out of parks at night. You could always be mistaken for a member of an opposing gang or get caught in a gang fight."

Anthropologists do not always avoid danger. Violence, war, and brutalities are realities of human behavior and well deserving of study. But anthropologists who undertake these studies are well aware of the issues of ethics and responsibility—most importantly to safeguard the lives of their collaborators. It is usual to meet with collaborators at different and secret locations, and never to be seen with them in public or visit their homes or workplaces. In extreme cases, anthropologists have arranged for collaborators and their families to be whisked out of the country.

Another consideration is medical care and medical evacuation. Make sure you are covered for both. Some universities now require their graduate students to have the proper health insurance coverage and will even cover the cost. Also make sure you are vaccinated and carry with you appropriate medications as preventatives or in case of emergencies. Some physicians will prescribe pills and give instructions on their use in the field. That said, local physicians will be better trained to diagnose local diseases. It is suggested that anthropologists seek out a physician who has served or trained in the country where they have been doing research, in case they become ill within a few months of returning home.

Chapter Four

The Perceiver and the Perceived

BEING THE OBJECT

When you enter the field it is with the purpose of observing and learning about others. You are prepared, with notebook in back pocket or iPad at hand, to scrutinize and note the behavior of those around you—and, eventually, to make some sense of it all. What may come as a surprise is the scrutiny *you* receive, everywhere you go. Tierney writes of her surprise and how she "felt uncomfortable . . . when the tables were turned and people on the street took to watching me . . . I was the oddity on the street . . I was being observed and scrutinized with as much intensity as I myself employed while watching them" (2007: 10).

One of the hardest things to do is to put yourself in a situation where you will be ridiculed, considered stupid. "But you have to open yourself up in ways you are not in ordinary life. You have to open yourself up to being snubbed. You have to stop making points to show how 'smart assed' you are . . . you have to be willing to be a horse's ass" (Goffman 2001 [1989]: 156). My students were willing to put themselves in that vulnerable position, and in the end, it led to acceptance.

Previously we saw how one student experienced these feelings when she walked into an Irish bar. Another student's experience took place in a Filipino restaurant:

I walk through the tiny parking lot of . . . a home-style Filipino restaurant, my legs are tired, my feet are sore, and my stomach hungry. I'd been walking around Historic Filipino town for the last two hours and taking notes on my impressions of the place. . . . I walked into the restaurant proper and found . . . I could not understand a word of any conversation because everyone was speaking Tagalog . . . I was the only white guy here; this was a strange experience for me, and I had been having it all day. I have never felt like so much of an outsider . . . sitting here in [the restaurant] eating lunch I am getting second looks from everyone who walks in or out of the place! It was a little disconcerting being looked at like this and I hadn't expected it . . . in fact the Filipinos that I know personally have always been very friendly and welcoming. I thought back and the only person that had been friendly towards me during this trip to Historic Filipino town had been a middle-aged Latino man who was drinking out of a brown paper bag as I passed him on the street; he said hello and wished me a good Valentine's Day.

Yet another student was also surprised to find himself treated as an outsider when he walked into a food market in Monterey Park, an enclave of recent Chinese immigrants:

To my surprise when I entered the store the two people behind the counter and the people they were helping stopped talking and looked straight at me. I said hello and gave them a smile to help break the ice. They then proceeded to continue talking to each other as if I were not there. This made me feel as if they were looking at me as an outsider and to be honest made me feel a little uncomfortable. I kept on looking around the store. . . . Once I reached the other side of the shop a woman of about 60 years old saw me looking very out of place and asked if I could use some help.

NOTHING IS NEUTRAL

When entering the field site for the first time, anthropologists will look for neutral topics to pursue as a way to ease into the community and not cause alarm. It is a good way of establishing trust before delving into topics that might be controversial or sensitive. But anthropologists will tell you that finding neutral topics is not always easy. What is considered neutral in one culture can be a quagmire in another. "Kinship," who is related to whom, and "land use," which are your gardens or fields and what crops you grow, are two topics traditionally considered neutral starts. They also have the advantage of not requiring one to intrude into people's homes. And they are a good way to get to know everyone and how they are related. But even here, one must tread lightly and not assume.

People can become suspicious of questions about the names and ages of their children, especially of young women and men. There might fear that the government is making lists of military-age males and that their young men will be recruited or forcefully removed. This, in turn, can lead to suspicions that the anthropologist might be an agent of the government. Male anthropologists who ask questions about females of marriageable age also come under suspicion of their motives and interest in the young women of the village. Young men who might be of military age and young women of marriageable age may be sent to stay safely with relatives in neighboring villages until the anthropologist leaves. In some cultures just asking about names is problematic: It is considered an insult to mention the names of certain members of the culture to their face or to their close relatives. In other cultures it is taboo to mention the names of the deceased. Questions concerning crops and land might also be interpreted negatively, casting suspicion that the anthropologist is a spy sent by the government to assess taxes on crop productions for individual households.

TRUST AND THE ETHICS OF FIELDWORK

How one is perceived can lead to ethical questions of conduct. You do not want to misrepresent or pass yourself off as someone you are not. I tell my students that they must be open about who they are and what they are doing; that is, they are college students who want to learn about and understand other cultures. When I was handed a paper written by a student in my anthropology class on gender, a short study comparing male and female police officer behavior, I was taken aback. It was an excellent piece, but how did he manage to get invited to "ride along" in the patrol car for an afternoon? Perhaps he had been introduced by a close friend? Or was he related to one of the police officers? When asked, he replied that he had told the officers that he was a newspaper reporter working on a story about police officers! Needless to say that story is told in every class I have taught since—as an example of how *not* to behave. But this issue is not as clear-cut as it first appears, and we will address its complexities in the following pages.

The American Anthropological Association has formulated guidelines for a code of ethics that includes the problem outlined above (AAA 2012). And "guidelines" is the operative word. The anthropologist in the field will encounter situations often faced by anthropologists in any field site, but each situation will also be unique. First and foremost, no harm must come to those one studies. This means anonymity for the subjects and constraint in what is reported in publications. These rules are *ironclad*. People anthropologists study are often at risk if their identities become known, particularly those living in areas torn by violence, in totalitarian states, and the like. Anyone going into the field needs to consult the AAA Code of Ethics on the AAA website. But be cautioned—the code is still being debated within the academy and it is subject to change.

The road from suspicion to trustworthiness is a rocky one. Establishing trust is fundamental to doing fieldwork. But once trust is established, secrets will emerge. Secrets that could (and indeed have been known to) threaten a people's safety. Once trust is established, the anthropologist may gain knowledge that is crucial to understanding behavior, but to reveal that knowledge could put the population at risk of exploitation, even eradication. This may appear to be a dilemma, but according to the American Anthropological Association's Code of Ethics, there is only one course of action—inaction.

Glenn Peterson writes:

> Secrecy, constraint, and caution are of the utmost importance to almost all the peoples anthropologists work with. To learn from them, one has to be not only respectful but also trustworthy—to keep one's mouth shut when necessary. . . . The rub, of course, is that what an ethnographer is apt to learn when he or she is quiet may well be extremely confidential, and that leads to what I think of as the central contradiction of ethnographic work: The more useful information is to our work and to our careers, the more likely it is that making use of it will pose a threat to those from whom we've learned it. (This is hardly unique to ethnography—for journalists and lawyers grapple with the same dilemma). We must forever balance our data, our careers, and the rights and well-being of the people we study. In the end, it's the people who must come first. (Peterson 2012: B20)

TENACITY

You are not the first stranger to your site. People will judge you—either positively or negatively—based on their experiences with previous visitors. You will want to be aware of how you are being treated and try to discover why. Villagers were suspicious of Julia Grunenfelder because they were used to nongovernment organizations (NGOs), and NGOs only visited once every two months and they brought questionnaires. Grunenfelder, on the other hand, visited frequently and just talked to people, who were uncomfortable with this unaccustomed behavior and initially asked her to leave (2014). My own experience working in the Mexican archives can be used as an example of initial suspicion. My Mexican research assistant instructed me to identify myself as a historian, not an anthropologist. When pressed as to why, she replied that people would not understand why an anthropologist was looking at documents rather than the local community. It was six months later, after we had established a relationship based on trust, that she finally gave me the real reason—it would be assumed that an American anthropologist doing research in Latin America would be working for the CIA, which in some circles would close the door to research.

Or you may just be thought to be dumb. Ernestine Friedl wrote that Powdermaker often told anecdotes about her fieldwork at parties and relates the following:

> One night when people from a visiting community were in the village, Powdermaker overheard the visiting chief ask the local chief what the white woman was doing in their midst. The chief replied that she was fine now, no trouble. But at first, he explained, she had been hopeless. She didn't know anything. She was like a child. She couldn't speak and she didn't have sense enough not to sit under a coconut tree. Now she was a reasonable human being, and, he ended proudly, "We taught her everything she knows." (Friedl 1991: 477).

Imposed Identity/Negotiated Identity

How one presents oneself and how one is perceived are complicated. How one represents oneself and one's research is often out of the control of the anthropologist. Presenting yourself in an open and honest manner does not mean there will be no misunderstandings. People will construct an identity for an outsider, such as an anthropologist, that fits with their own worldview, that those in the culture feel most comfortable with, that "makes sense." Anthropologists have often chosen to accept that identity, when not accepting that identity will bring offense and especially when it affords a measure of safety. Margaret Mead allowed others to believe she was married when being unmarried was either unacceptable or unimaginable. No amount of explaining satisfied those who asked why Margaret Mead, at her age, was unmarried and without children. So she took to wearing a wedding ring. Others have negotiated an identity that seems to best fit the situation and smooth the way for fieldwork. In the end, it is up to the anthropologist to decide when to correct and when to just accept—and when to negotiate a new role.

Matthews Masayuki Hamabata first entered his field site in Japan as a graduate student in his 20s. Hamabata was brought up in the United States as an Americanized third-generation Japanese. His outward appearance, which was indistinguishable from the Japanese he was studying, brought the expectation of behavior appropriate for a Japanese male. But it quickly became evident that he did not know how to behave. Because of his limited language skills and inability to navigate the complex rules of behavior required of an adult, he was initially treated as a young boy. This was awkward for him, but as he became more proficient at practicing Japanese cultural traits and thus was perceived as a young Japanese man, he found himself in an even more awkward position. His unmarried state as a young Japanese man made him the ideal marriage partner for the daughters of his interviewees. Refusing to be considered for an arranged marriage put him in an uncomfortable position, and it threatened to derail his research. First, it diminished his worthiness—he was told that it was "undutiful" (1991: 15) to his parents not to agree to an arranged marriage. Second, he was now considered arrogant—did he refuse to marry into a prominent Japanese family because he considered his own family better than theirs? His solution was to revert back to the status of an immature male by referring to himself as a boy, acting naïve about adult matters, and even preferring candy to scotch. He renegotiated a position for himself, the same position that had initially been imposed upon him by others, to save his research project (1991).

While in the field, Stephen David Siemens and his wife, Wendy Rader, did not "act" as a married couple in the manner required by the Azande culture. In particular, Wendy did not conform to traditional gender roles. She would accompany her husband to gatherings where only males socialized. She did not plant, cultivate, and cook for him. Because the Azande could not fit either member of the couple into appropriate native roles, they imposed roles for the couple that would make sense in their culture. They concluded that she was not really his wife but that they had been sent out by their school together so neither would be lonely (Siemens 1993).

Drawing on Your Life Experiences

Anderson writes (2000: 3), "Fieldwork classes prepare us for what to do, and that training is crucial. What we can less adequately be prepared for is how we internalize the field experience," in other words, how we draw on our life experiences and emotions to understand this new world we have chosen to study. But it is important that anthropologists be aware of how we translate what is observed through the prism of "self." We bring to the field site life experiences and a value system that can be both a boon and a hindrance, in ways that are hard to anticipate but are crucial to understand. We need to be aware of the limitations of our own worldviews in order not to let them color our perceptions of others. But our life experiences can also be the bridge that affords an entrée into another culture.

We have already met the student whose research brought her to an Irish bar. Her cousin was British—"and when I was a kid brought me up on European football." This turned out to be her entrée:

> So I walked over to the bar counter where three people . . . were all facing the screen and chanting out screams of support for the team while tossing their beer mugs around (as I have only seen . . . in movies). With the courage that I now sort of obtained I took a step toward them and started to talk shop. At first they were a little puzzled that I might know about football but did not exactly reject my meeting with them. After a brief moment for them to take me all in, I began a dialog introducing myself to them, telling them my mission and assignment. I finished watching the game with them and as I turned to leave was given an invitation to drop by again "if I had the time."

Her knowledge of soccer opened the door.

Another student brought to the field her knowledge of ginseng. "Throughout Chinatown there are shops, shops and more shops. . . . Within any one of these, you can find tons of ginseng roots. What I found interesting is that *every last bit of* ginseng was of the American kind. Due to my job, which specializes in supplements, I know that American ginseng is not the best type. Better kinds are Siberian, Chinese or Korean." My student returned to Chinatown and her persistence paid off. She found the higher quality (and greatly more expensive) ginseng on a second floor of a shop where tourists were absent and discovered a part of Chinatown she might have otherwise missed.

WHAT YOU TAKE FROM THE FIELD CHANGES YOU

Kenneth Read (see chapter 1) discovered, in the field, he had personal resources "that I had doubted I possessed" (1965: 9), that he could be alone without others of his own culture for a long period of time. More important, he had difficulty making close attachments in England, where he lived, and always blamed himself. When he made close attachments among the natives in Tofmora village in New Guinea, he realized it was not his own failures that prevented him from feeling accepted at home.

One student wrote she had to overcome shyness in order to make rapport. "[I learned that] if I wanted to proceed doing fieldwork some aspects of my personality had to change. . . . I allowed intimidation [to] take the best part of me and it affected my fieldwork experience. As a shy person, I realized that to create a more comfortable experience with this enclave, it had to be *me* who initiated the conversation."

Entrée and Acceptance

Entrée and acceptance are different stages of field research. Entrée is essentially being allowed to move in to a field site. Acceptance is when you become a part of your field site's community and it begins to interact with you. Acceptance into a community cannot to be taken for granted. It is rare for an anthropologist to suddenly appear in a community with no introduction: Someone in authority will most likely have provided a letter (or email) of introduction. But being allowed entrée and being accepted are two different things. It is the latter that leads to successful research. Initially, you will probably be seen with suspicion. Once the initial suspicion wears off, you can expect to be tolerated or ignored. And then, when least expected, you will make some gesture, or remark, and cross the threshold into acceptance. You have to be on the lookout for this moment because your acceptance by the group (or by the individual) will be marked by a gesture or remark displayed by (one of) them, which is often hard to read. So it's important to have your antennas up.

Recognizing gestures of acceptance can be difficult. Nor is it always possible to anticipate what gestures on your part will open doors. Anderson gives examples of both. The homes in the French village she studied were not easy to penetrate—fenced in and guarded by vicious dogs (2000: 77). And once inside, it was still not always possible to know if she was being accepted into the community or tolerated as a guest. The subtle gesture that marked her acceptance was the glass of wine she was offered at the home of the French villager she had come to interview. The action that opened the door was being a nursing mother: "My status did get a boost. . . . Word had it that American women were rarely so inclined and even when so disposed were seldom sufficiently endowed to do the job" (2000: 78).

Clifford and Hildred Geertz did fieldwork in Bali. Clifford Geertz, in a famous essay "Deep Play: Notes on the Balinese Cockfight," wrote of the dramatic transformation from entrée to acceptance. They had made arrangements to live in a small village but once they moved in, it became apparent that they were being treated as nonpersons, as invisible, ignored by the villagers. Not an auspicious way to start fieldwork. People were not rude; they just did not acknowledge them and would look past them if addressed. About 10 days after they arrived, the village held a cockfight, which drew a large crowd. It was also illegal. What followed was a police raid, which sent the crowd, including anthropologists, running in all directions. When the Geertzes saw a villager duck into a compound, they followed, and by the time a policeman came into the yard, four people were sitting at a covered table calmly drinking tea. Rather than just producing their papers for the police, they had fled with the rest and thus had allied themselves with the villagers. Overnight the Geertzes became visible and accepted. From then on, fieldwork became possible (Geertz 1973).

Fieldwork Is Serendipity

A famous quote attributed to the chemist Louis Pasteur is "chance favors the prepared mind." In many cases, successful fieldwork is built on unplanned opportunities. Powdermaker was invited to join the Lesu women in Melanesia who were practicing a dance they would perform at an upcoming gathering of tribes. At first she declined, because she felt self-conscious. But boredom soon set in, as night after night, the dancers went through their steps, and so, without thinking of the consequences, she joined in. The day of the celebration arrived, and much to her chagrin, she found she was expected to participate with the other dancers. With trepidation she set forth, but when she saw 12,000 natives at the gathering her resolve almost vanished. Then "the drums began. . . . Something happened. I forgot myself and was one with the dancers" (1993: 88). This was an important turning point in her fieldwork. "From then on the quality of my relationship with the women was different. I had their confidence as I had not had it before" (1993: 88). Even men were more forthcoming with invitations and information.

A student researching the Tongan community in the United States also found dance to be a watershed moment. After sitting on a bench watching a group of Tongan high school girls practice a dance for an upcoming event, she was persuaded to join in. Reluctantly she agreed. "I tried to hide in the back but was quickly spotted and pulled to the front." She was patiently put through the steps, accompanied by smiles of encouragement and good-natured laughter. As with Powerdermaker's experience, the girls opened up—about what dancing meant to them and about the importance of dancing to keep the Tongan culture alive.

Another student chose Little India as an ethnic enclave to study. She described how she was drawn to a shop by the beautiful saris displayed in the window. As she walked from table to table, fingering the delicate silks, she felt that her presence was being ignored. Only when she made a casual remark about her approaching wedding did things turned around. The shop keeper was also getting married! Conversation began with animated talk of wedding preparations and was soon followed by ready answers to any questions my student had.

INSIDER/OUTSIDER

Simply put, an insider is a member of the culture being studied, having been brought up with its norms and beliefs; an outsider is one who is not, who was brought up in a different culture. What are the advantages and disadvantages of each for the fieldworker? One is likely to assume that the "insider" has a distinct advantage; that is, statements and events are understandable within the broader context of a culture the researcher has known intimately since childhood. As an insider, one is less likely to feel ignorant or alone. The outsider-researcher may look with some envy on the insider—as one who will have an easier time and be more likely to do fruitful work. But as my students and many anthropologists have written, the insider faces obstacles not encountered by the outsider. For one thing, cultural frictions might place the insider in awkward positions.

Maxine Baca Zinn addresses the insider/outsider issue from her experience doing research on Chicano families she was able to access by affiliating herself with a community agency working with

Chicana mothers. Her dilemma was that she was seen as both insider and outsider. As a Chicana she was readily accepted by staff members as one of them. In fact, they lauded her research, saying more research was needed on Chicana women and should be done by Chicanas like herself. But there was a barrier she could not bridge—of class and education—until it became known that she did not know how to sew. The unequal status of educated Chicana researcher and working-class Chicana mothers was then reversed as the mothers teased Baca Zinn for her ineptitude in the use of a sewing machine and took on the role of instructor to novice. But being accepted as an insider can lead to its own problems. Once accepted, Baca Zinn found herself in the situation of being asked to intervene and act as advocate when a problem or misunderstanding arose between a mother and a staff member. Not able to refuse, this nonetheless put Baca Zinn in a precarious position that could have jeopardized her research (2001).

The distinction between insider and outsider is not always clear-cut. When I entered the field in Mexico I was seen as an American (or *gringa*, the slang term commonly used), an "outsider." But I was also the wife of someone treated like an "insider," my Cuban-born husband. This ambiguity became clear when we attended a function. Upon entering the room, my husband was greeted warmly, but some bristled at the presence of a *gringa*. "That's alright," I overheard someone say, "she's his wife." Insider/outsider—I was perceived as both.

A graduate student I knew found himself in a similarly ambiguous position. But he was able to move back and forth. He was a Samoan prince, son of a chief in a village where Margaret Mead had done her fieldwork. When he regaled his fellow graduate students with stories of "Maggie," he was clearly an "insider" from his village, and we were the outsiders. But as a fellow graduate student, he was also an "insider." He was going through the same "rituals" of coursework, doctoral exams, and dissertation writing that were part and parcel of the training to become an anthropologist—he was "one of us."

Chapter Five

Theory

USE WITH CAUTION

In "A Scandal in Bohemia" in *The Adventures of Sherlock Holmes*, Arthur Conan Doyle has Sherlock Holmes warn that it's "a capital mistake to theorize before one has data. Insensibly one begins to twist facts to suit theories, instead of theories to suit facts." This was published in 1892 and still rings true today (2010 [1892]: 163).

What is a theory? Depending on the context, the word "theory" can refer to anything from a simple speculation to a well-established and accurate depiction of the nature of things. In science, a theory is a set of general rules about some aspect of the world, based on observation and used to explain, predict, and organize the subject matter in question, as well as to point to new avenues of research. For instance, Newton's theory of gravitation explains an enormous variety of phenomena, such as why objects fall and how fast, and even the paths of planets. The theory of evolution explains the nature of biological species, their diversity, and their similarities. As scientists observe more and collect more facts, a theory must be tested and revised, and even discarded if it fails to correctly match the observations. Progress in science is often linked to replacing an old theory with one that is more predictive or explanatory, and this is an ongoing process.

A theory helps one to organize and understand the data. But an entrenched theory can also blind one and lead to false conclusions. Going into the field with a preconceived theory is a double-edged sword. A theory can structure what one sees: It can explain and give context to what is being observed. It can open one's eyes and be broadening. But used poorly, it can be a straightjacket. If everything you observe, if all your data, is forced to fit a particular theory, at best this will not lead to new insights, and at worst it can bias or distort your analysis.

An example of how adhering to theory can hinder understanding comes from Renato Rosaldo in his essay "Grief and a Headhunter's Rage" (1993). Rosaldo and his wife Michelle Rosaldo were living with and studying the Filipino Ilongots. This was a group that had practiced headhunting, and Rosaldo sought to understand why. An elder explained that grief from loss propelled men to take a human head: "The act of severing and tossing away the victim's head enables him, he says, to vent and, he hopes, throw away the anger of his bereavement. . . . To him, grief, rage, and headhunting go together in a self-evident manner" (1993: 1). Expressions of grief in the Western world, Rosaldo's world, took many forms, but headhunting was not one of them. Having seen no similar behavior in the Western world, and not having experienced such personal grief himself, Rosaldo concluded that there must be another, truer explanation, of which the Ilongots were unaware. Exchange theory seemed to fit. Applying this theory, Rosaldo would posit that "one death canceled another" (3). Even when one elder remarked that some might think so, but that wasn't why they did it, Rosaldo still held fast to the theory. And then tragedy struck. Rosaldo's wife, walking a muddy path, slipped and fell down a steep ravine to her death. Rosaldo had equated loss only with pain until he experienced loss himself—and the ensuing rage. Western cultures do not acknowledge rage, he concluded; it is the Ilongots who acknowledged its presence.

Use theories wisely. It's good to keep them in mind; they can be very useful. Take from them new ways of thinking; use them to question what you see; try them on and see if they fit. Do they help explain what you are observing? Or does what you are observing not really fit? Theories have excellent explanatory powers when constructed well and applied judiciously. But remember, the field is pushed forward when new data bring a theory into question.

THE DEBATE ON SCIENCE AND HUMANITY

Theories do not have to be seen as either/or. Two seemingly opposing views may well be two sides of the same coin. This is true of the science/humanity debate. Much has been made of the debates between those who view anthropology as part of the humanities and those who emphasize the science in the social science that is anthropology. Those who view anthropology as a science require that the anthropologist be a neutral observer of human behavior, collecting empirical data, similar to the chemist in the lab or the physicist formulating equations. Anthropologists as humanists do not see themselves as neutral, but rather as individuals who bring their own life experiences and worldviews to the field site, which colors what they see. Rather than being neutral observers, they are seen as having an influence on those they study, which in turn influences the data collection and how it is interpreted. Those who view anthropology as part of the humanities are likely to use subjective terms such as intuition, imagination, interpretation, reflexivity while scientific articles are sprinkled with such objective words as empirical data, logical analysis, generalizations, and testable hypotheses. For the former, it is an interpretation of events, for the latter the description of physical facts.

For some anthropologists, the two approaches are irreconcilable, and for a few these differences have escalated from debate to outright war. But most anthropologists now view these two approaches as complimentary and necessary for a full understanding of human behavior. This can best be summed up by a quote often attributed to Eric Wolf (although it has been attributed to others as well). Anthropology is "the most scientific of the humanities, and the most humanistic of the sciences."

PART 2

METHODS

Chapter Six

Participant-Observation

In the field, the anthropologist is both participant and observer. Here we look at the tensions between these two roles: the role of participant, of closeness, where one takes part in activities and becomes involved, and the role of observer, where one stands back and watches closely. Juggling these two roles and your position in the community is an ongoing process and not one that can always be taught. In the 1930s, when students at Yale University asked for a course in field methodology, they were told that the topic was fine for breakfast conversation but not serious material for instruction (Bernard 2011). Today most anthropology majors are required to take a course in methodology, and you may be reading this book for such a class. But there is still much that goes unsaid, that anthropologists still consider unteachable.

PARTICIPANT-OBSERVATION: IT CAN'T ALWAYS BE TAUGHT

The DeWalts write that how we learn to understand another culture is a process that is hard to convey in words. Some, they say, would describe it as understanding on the level of the body—learning to move, sit, and eat, as we share the lives of others. This way of learning how to behave can result in learning what life means to the people we study. And since participant-observation means interacting with others and reacting to others, teaching students about what to do and how to do it in specific situations is not possible, because not everything you encounter in the field can be anticipated (DeWalt and DeWalt 2011). Jean Jackson calls participant-observation "ethnography-by-the-seat-of-your-pants" (Jackson 1990b: 25). What can be taught is to be aware that this will be the case and to be prepared for it. This was illustrated in a class I attended with Professor Allen Johnson whose work among the Machiguenga is well-known. He put a slide on the screen of a man lying on the ground under a tree, eyes wide open. What is he doing, he asked us? "Resting from vigorous activity," "going to sleep," "thinking," were some of our answers. No, said Dr. Johnson. He is doing *nothing*, he is just lying there doing nothing and thinking about nothing. It was a concept unfamiliar to us in the West, where we are always doing something, or feel that we should be. Dr. Johnson could not have learned to recognize this "activity" in a classroom. He had to learn it in the field. And it was also too foreign for us to recognize. What we did learn was not to assume, and to expect the unexpected. That said, you still can be prepared.

Some simple things to keep in mind:

- **Choosing a site:** Choose an easy site if you are just beginning. Leave the outlaw biker club for a more seasoned investigator. As we have said earlier, the familiar will be difficult enough.

- **Preparing beforehand:** Write up something you can present to people that outlines what you will be doing, but make it vague enough so you will not show your hand or paint yourself into a corner—things will change. Then rehearse how you will explain it.

- **Overcoming biases:** We all have biases; we can't eliminate them. But we can acknowledge our biases, become aware of them, and work to not let these feelings influence how we view others.

- **Being flexible and open to surprises:** You will have a goal for your research, but be open to surprises that may suggest new, unanticipated directions for your research to take, or the importance of an event otherwise thought to be unimportant. Adler and Adler (cited in Angrosino 2007) spoke of this as the "'Click!' experience," which they describe as "a sudden, though minor, epiphany as to the emotional depth or importance of an event or a phenomenon." Note it; then ponder its meaning and how it might redirect your research.

WHAT IS PARTICIPANT-OBSERVATION?

Participant-observation is not just about living in proximity—missionaries and traders did that. Or only about collecting data. It is a way of thinking about people, and about how one perceives one's own position in relation to the people one is studying. It is watching, doing, listening. It is observing and participating in the daily life of people. It is "immersing yourself in a culture . . . [and] learning to act so that people go about their business as usual" (Bernard 2011:258).

Some simple things to keep in mind:

- **Ordinary participation and "participation"/observation are different:** We participate and we observe on a daily basis. But we zone out much of what is happening around us if it does not concern us. If you are standing in line at the grocery store, are you noticing everything around you? Or are you thinking of something else? Barbara Monsey (cited in Spradley 2016 [1980]: 55) tells us, as anthropologists, to "force [yourself] to pay attention to information . . . normally excluded." James Spradley calls it "explicit awareness" (Spradley 2016 [1980]: 55).

- **Participant-observation—a continuum:** As a passive observer, you are a bystander, as when you are observing by sitting in a criminal court. In moderate participation your presence is known but you are still only watching. In complete participation, such as playing pool, you are actively doing what others are doing. In each of these cases your relationship with the observed changes from outsider to closeness. In all cases, you are learning cultural rules (Spradley 2016 [1980]).

- **Importance of participation:** Participation gives us an understanding of the people we study that is different from what we learn by observing. "As your hands blister from the hoe handle, as you drink the beer then learn to serve it when appropriate, you learn some of the small imponderables that are hard to put into words but far, far harder to elicit. Knowing them, other things become comprehensible. Your understanding somewhat improved" (Zeitlyn 2003: 68).

- **The tension between maintaining closeness and distance:** If you immerse yourself, for example, by becoming a taxi driver or a member of a band, you will need to move back and forth between participation (which brings firsthand knowledge of the insider's view) and observation (with the insight that comes from being more objective and analyzing a situation). One solution posited by Hong and Duff (2002) is to work as a team, where one researcher participates more and the other observes more. But maintaining either of these positions is not always under your control. Your subject may demand more closeness, or resist it (Emerson 2001: 241), and you may find yourself having trouble negotiating your place, which can cause stress.

Bernard would argue that participant-observation "involves deception," and he says that if that "sounds a bit crass, it is meant to" (Bernard 2011: 256). I have heard other anthropologists question if what they do is transparent enough to those they study. Thus it is important to think of the ethics of our behavior while we are in the field. One concern is how we are perceived. We may think we have been clear about who we are, what we are doing, and what we plan to do with the data we gather. But are these things understood by those we study? It is our responsibility to make sure that they are. And are there situations where you do not have to reveal your identity? What if you are just visiting and the conversation turns to something you are currently researching? You want to use this information. Now you need to take on the role of anthropologist, being transparent about what you are doing, asking permission to use what has been revealed, and talking about confidentiality. This is tricky and can be awkward. You need to be open about the fact that you are studying others and continually reassess that relationship to make sure it is clear (Musante 2014).

HOW TO LEARN

It may be harder to learn about your own culture because we don't notice what is familiar to us. Bernard gives as an example the middle-class American cultural trait of grazing rather than sitting down to a meal. Would you notice that, he asks? We need to learn by becoming a novice, seeing things as if they were new (Bernard 2015).

Learning to See, Not Just Look

My students all wrote about how they learned to make this transition. One student is a member of the San Pedro community, home also to Croatian immigrants. Even though she lives in the area, she writes, "I was taken aback to see how much [of the neighborhood] had Croatian origins that I always overlooked . . . [restaurants, shops, a cultural center], these places went under my radar before this project. . . . It's funny how much you miss just because you're not looking for it." Another student said, "Although to the untrained eye, it is just another city block with shops and restaurants, if you are looking you will see that all of these shops are for an Indian demographic. Walking past the open doors you could hear all the music from the Bollywood films, and smell the delicious smells coming from the grocery shops and restaurants."

Another student wrote about how she learned the importance of seeing: "In the midst of writing my essay I realized that I didn't have enough information to write . . . much about the market. I wasn't able to analyze everything because I hadn't paid enough attention to small details. This made me learn that you really have to pay attention to the small things when you are doing an ethnography, that those small things can be of big importance." As a student noted, "It can take time to really see." Another student wrote that she was disappointed there "was no structure to the neighborhood that was obvious[ly] Cambodian . . . that Cambodian presence was not visible. [But] as the semester went on and I went back several times to get a little closer, I noticed that there [actually] was a lot of Cambodian culture, with the small markets." This was also true for a student studying Koreatown: "When I walked through the streets . . . I realized that Koreatown was divided into two different categories—[upscale] Korean-owned chain businesses and [local] family-owned businesses appeared to be located on smaller less attractive streets. It took me a while to notice this."

Learning How to Behave

You try to be discreet and try to blend while looking at how others are behaving, all the time worrying that you will look foolish, or worse, will offend. One student describes the first time he sat down to eat a meal in an Ethiopian restaurant in Los Angeles:

> As I waited for my meal the first sign and symptom of culture shock began . . . as I noticed the other people eating didn't use any forks, knives, or spoons . . . in this peculiar position of not knowing what to do I just focused in . . . on how the other customers ate their meal. With a false yawn here and a scratching of the beard there all in an effort not to look directly at [those nearest to me in order to learn] how to conduct myself at the table.

THE RELATIONSHIP BETWEEN
ANTHROPOLOGIST AND SUBJECT

Developing Rapport

People have to be comfortable with you before they will open up. "Hanging out" is one way to gain rapport (Bernard 2014: 368). This allows you to learn enough about the culture to ask questions, especially sensitive ones, so that they are not offensive or sound stupid. Rapport involves respect, being a good listener, and being ready to reciprocate, both in material ways and about one's personal life. This can be tricky, for example if you are asked about political views when yours differ from your collaborators' views. Being vague or general may be one way to answer. And confidentiality is essential—never talk about others or reveal what they told you. They will learn about what you say even if you don't share it with them (DeWalt and DeWalt 2011).

The Observed and the Observer

Tierney writes that participant-observation is "always a joint effort" and emphasizes there needs to be mutual respect and the process must be enjoyable for both the researcher and the researched (2007: 16). This is easier for some than for others—it depends on the situation and the persons involved. One anthropologist said in an interview, "I found [troubling] the very peculiar experience [of] getting to know people; becoming their friend, their confidant, and to be at the same time standing on the side and observing" (quoted in Jackson 1990b: 18). When the line between collaborator and friend blurs, how much of what he/she tells you can you use, publish? And there is also the risk of being hurt. For example, closeness may mean hearing about violence and abuse. "Childhood stories of violently forced sex," says Bourgois, "spun me into a personal depression and a research crisis" (cited in Bernard 2011: 277). And you will be tested. When someone asks what you may know about another person—you say you don't know anything!

Distancing Yourself

When accompanying the social worker to a home crisis, an anthropologist deliberately sat apart, concentrating on note taking so as not to be drawn into the confrontation. When asked to take sides, the anthropologist tried to find something positive to say about both. Invited out on a date by a collaborator, the anthropologist declined, using overwork as an excuse.

Gatekeepers

A gatekeeper is a person who tries to control access to or information about a group. Gatekeepers are common in fieldwork situations (Schensul and LeCompte cited in Musante 2014: 265). If a marginalized member of society tries to be a gatekeeper, the anthropologist needs to distance him/herself without offending, or risk being marginalized as well. However, some gatekeepers are protecting their domain. If the gatekeeper is someone of authority in the group you want to study, then a relationship needs to be established. Permission may need to be sought before beginning. A student who was studying gender behavior in a grocery store was questioned about his motive by the manager of the grocery store when he began to jot notes near the cash registers where, the manager pointed out, thousands of dollars passed hands. When he explained his project, permission was granted. But he should have approached the manager first.

Never the Native

David Hayano, in *Poker Faces,* claims he became so immersed in the subculture of poker players that "within several years I had virtually become one of the people I wanted to study" (Hayano 1982: 149). But anthropologists debate about whether they ever truly become native, especially when they continue the role of researching anthropologist. Powdermaker describes this when she writes of her participation in the ritual dance with the Lesu women in Melanesia. "Under the full moon and for the brief time of the dance, I ceased to be an anthropologist from a modern society. I danced. When it was over I realized that, for this short period, I had been emotionally part of the rite. Then out came my notebook" (1993: 88).

Some anthropologists need to take on a near native position for their studies. The anthropologist who studies shamanism hopes to be invited to train as a shaman by those he/she is studying. Others accept the roles of fictive kin, such as daughter or son. But these roles come with obligations and responsibilities, and it is important to consider carefully before taking one on (Musante 2014).

Unequal Status

Anthropologists question whether fieldwork can ever really mean equality between the observers and the observed. You have a privileged position as a researcher, but you can also be useful to others, which gives them leverage. Some have complained that natives were only cooperative in exchange for tobacco, pills, or other goods obtainable only from the anthropologist. But providing needed goods and services is also a responsibility of your position. For example, an anthropologist in a small Mexican village owned the only van, which was used as both a bus and an ambulance and was often in demand. And there are times when the anthropologist has the opportunity to contribute by designing a collaborative project. Elizabeth Enslin's PhD is such a project. The women in a Nepalese village wanted to become literate. Because there was no safe place for them to study, the anthropologist aided them in building a women's center for this and other activities (cited in Wolf 1992: 124). In fact, anthropologists have been helping artisans form cooperatives and facilitating the marketing of their goods for some time. Grimes and Milgram (2000) have edited a book that documents the role of anthropologists as agents for groups of artisans.

Gender, Age, and Class

Be on the lookout for areas that may be closed to you due to your gender, age, class, or other factors; know how to recognize them and how to get around them. Know that you may not be seeing everything and how to ask and who to ask about what may be hidden. For example, three female anthropologists in rural Kentucky, after months in the field, were visited by a friend who was a male anthropologist. The first question their local male collaborator asked the visitor was if he was a drinking man. Although the female anthropologists had worked in the community, they had never been aware that whiskey was being made in their midst. Because they were women, it was never mentioned (DeWalt, DeWalt, and Wayland 2000: 280). On the other hand, gender does not always limit access. As mentioned above, when Siemens showed interest in Azante women's rituals he had no trouble documenting these important rites, which were unknown to the male anthropologist who had done work previously in the village (Siemens 1993).

WHAT TO OBSERVE

Be aware of *daily life,* special and/or unusual events, people—their gestures, conversations, expressions, actions, and reactions—

space, colors, smells, sounds. In familiar places we need to make an effort to notice the things that go on around us that we usually ignore. In unfamiliar places we need to understand the function and importance of things that are new to us.

You have to recognize the various *sounds* and what they mean. When we first moved to Mexico we had to learn the meaning of sounds. If we did not recognize the honk that accompanied the water truck, which required us to go out and flag it down, we would not have potable water to drink. To have sharpened knives and scissors we needed to heed the sound of the pan flute that announced the scissor sharpener. For late-night snacks of tamales, it was the toot of the tamale vendor's cart. Sounds that started out as unfamiliar to us were an integral part of Mexican life.

In Western cultures *smells* are often considered offensive. Consider the large number of products, from body deodorants to car and house sanitizers, that are aimed at eradicating odors. To the newly arrived anthropologist, smells can be overwhelming, such as those emanating from sweaty bodies crammed into a small hut. Smells may have important functions and symbolic or other meanings that are unfamiliar to us but are an intrinsic part of the culture. For the Ongee of the Andaman Islands, one greets another by saying *"Konyune onorange-tanka?"* ("How is your nose?"). If the person says he/she is "heavy with odor," the greeter inhales deeply to remove some of the surplus. If the greeted person answers that she/he lacks odor, the greeter will politely let out a breath to provide some (Fox n.d.). But don't make assumptions about the meaning of scents. The burning of incense may have a religious purpose, for example to communicate with the spirit world; it may be used in a healing ceremony; or it may just be used to mask a musty home in Dakar (Suzanne Scheld personal communication 2014).

What people do and what they say they do are not always the same. In Bolivia, June Nash found that even though women worked, they saw themselves mainly as wives and mothers and only as men's helpers. It brought shame if a man could not support his family, so women would sneak out to do the work in the fields at night so no one would see them. They certainly would not talk about it (Nash and Safa 1986: 5). Martha Rees's findings in rural Oaxaca were similar. Throughout Mexico the males Rees asked told her women did not work in the fields, yet everywhere she went she saw women growing crops. She was also told men migrated north to work in the United States in order to support their families even though remittances were rare and it was women's work that made male migration possible (Rees 2006).

STUDYING DIVERSITY IN
LARGE URBAN ENVIRONMENTS

Students in my methodology class, each of whom had chosen as a field site an immigrant population within the city, were instructed to make a total of six visits to their field site: two visits where they kept on the move, walking and looking and getting an overview of the territory; two visits where they slowed down their pace to observe; and two visits where they stayed still and observed the world as it moved past them.

The First Two Visits: Walking through the Community

For the first two visits, students were told to look at the physical space—if in an enclave, they may want to map it. What is its size—large, small? Boundaries? How diverse is it (are shop signs in more than one language)? Who do the shops seem to cater to—members of the community or tourists? Sometimes evidence of an immigrant community is hidden, such as in restaurants and video stores where the foreign-language menus and videos are kept upstairs, while English-language menus and videos are on the main floor. Describe the feel of the place—quiet, noisy, slow-paced, or busy. How do you feel there? Some students may have chosen an immigrant population that is more scattered throughout the city. Rather than walking through a neighborhood, they had to drive around to find them. But they still got out of the car and walked around. The view changed closer up.

The first two visits were designed to ease students into the field, but they were told to still expect some anxiety, that this is normal. A student wrote, "Although the purpose of my initial visit concerned first impressions and the collecting of quantitative data I was nevertheless anxious regarding how the experience would unfold." Students wrote that on subsequent visits the fieldwork became easier.

Visits Three and Four: Slowing Down

For the next two visits, students were told to slow down a bit and observe more closely in one place, such as a commercial enterprise—for example, to walk around a shopping mall or a large market and to describe what is being sold and who is in the shop (employees and customers). Does the shop appear to be geared toward the local ethnic customer base—are most of the signs and the products' labels written in another language? Are the people shopping there speaking a foreign language? Do customers appear to know one another; that is, do they greet each other in a personal/familiar manner? Is it a tourist shop (and how do you know)? Are customers a mixed group? Are products also a mixed group, cornflakes next to a can with no English label? Does the shop play a function other than to sell; for example, is there a group of elderly men sitting around and talking (a place to socialize)? Are there free newsletters or magazines in a bin, and in what language? What is hanging on the walls—posters, flyers, a message board with cards pinned to it (networking or job seeking)? Does it serve as a post office (this is true for herbal shops in Chinatown in San Francisco)? Can you rent videos (in some Indian markets you can rent Bollywood videos in Hindi), buy books or newspapers, etc.? Again, in what language? Can you place overseas calls (this is true for some Indian and Mexican markets)? What is the "feel," the "vibe," of the store? How are you treated and how do you feel?

Students could ask people in the shop questions, if the occasion arose and it seemed appropriate, but it was not a necessary part of the assignment. In fieldwork, it is all about sizing up a situation and making a decision about what to do. Students learn that when they slow down, they see more. A student wrote:

> I discovered my first impressions were only the beginning or outer layer of the onion. . . . After my first two trips into the enclave I began to feel somewhat comfortable sitting down and simply allowing for the enclave to work while I observed. I began to notice how the individuals whom I determined to be regular visitors and those who were members of the community of Little Tokyo did not ignore me, but in some instances actively engaged me even if it was to simply hand me a flyer for one of the upcoming cultural events. This level of openness to my presence was not what I had previously thought of when considering the Japanese culture.

The Last Two Visits: Watching the World Move Past You

For visits five and six, students were told to stop and stay still, in one place, while the world revolves around you. This is yet another perspective that yields different types of data. The goal is to go where people gather—cultural centers, museums, cultural events, art exhibits, conferences, parks, restaurants, cafes. In Chinatown, the elderly congregate on park benches. In Russian enclaves, men gather in parks and cafés to play chess. Now you will be moving from observation to participation. You can initiate a conversation, but it is more likely that people will talk to you! One student, who had spent time in an Iranian market, returned and just sat on the steps. He said it was amazing how much he saw when he stopped moving and just observed.

Chapter Seven

Jottings

You are in the field—a homeless shelter, an Irish sports bar, a high school gym where Samoan-American girls are practicing a native dance—ready to observe and hoping to participate. You have put a notepad, a tablet, or a cell phone in your back pocket or backpack for note taking—for your *jottings*. Jottings, also called jot notes or scratch notes, are the brief notes made at the time of doing fieldwork—the notes that, when expanded, will become the field notes upon which publications are based.

This chapter discusses the importance of keeping an ongoing field notebook of your observations, impressions, and tentative explanations and personal feelings; of behaviors, body language, and pieces of conversations and specific words; of your sketches of places; and your descriptions of scents and sounds. It discusses how to handle the problem of juggling observing with note taking and how much (or little) to record. It suggests that each person develop a sort of personal shorthand, and it talks about writing down first impressions before they fade and the necessity to flesh out these notes as soon as possible before they become difficult to decipher. What appears at first to be unfamiliar soon becomes so familiar that you will no longer notice, and it will drop off your radar screen. George Stocking has observed that the field notebook has many uses beyond a place for taking notes, not least of which is that it serves as a safety valve (1983).

Students need to make a distinction between what they observe and how they interpret what they observe. Jottings are descriptions of what is going on. They can also include tentative explanations because we want to make sense of what we observe. But don't confuse "explanation" with "description." Roughly, a description tells you what, an explanation tells you why. Both are important, but they need to be kept separate. Distinction is a key here.

There is no one right way to do things. Of course there are things you should not do—most would agree with these and we mention them below. But whether you show members of the society your notes or not, and other aspects of taking notes, that will have to be negotiated in the field. And as you will see, for every opinion that A should be done, there will be an equal number of anthropologists arguing for B. Here you will be introduced to both sides, but in the field it is your call.

The topics below are by no means exhaustive, but they cover a lot of situations you might encounter in the field. This chapter is written so that you are aware of them before they happen and take you by surprise.

JOTTINGS: "HIDDEN AND MYSTERIOUS"

In the 1980s, there was little written on the subject of how to take notes in the field. Jackson found that "the literary canon (if we can speak thus) defining their form and content is extremely vague" (Jackson 1990a: 30), and James Clifford, who wrote a chapter for Sanjek's (1990a) edited book on field notes, lamented that "most of the actual practice and advice [about note-taking] is unrecorded or inaccessible" (Clifford 1990: 52).

Jackson (1990b) interviewed anthropologists to find out why so few people were writing about this important aspect of anthropological research. Many spoke of "our tendency to *avoid* talking about [taking notes] or only to *joke* about them (5) . . . or discuss them in 'corridor talk' or at parties" (10). She found reticence and unease on the subject. In fact, she doubted whether these anthropologists would publish some of what they told her, or if they would have talked to her at all if they thought she would publish it. Robert Emerson and Rachel Fretz found some anthropologists spoke of how unfinished their field notes are, how "messy" (Emerson, Fretz, and Shaw 2011: xv).

Many anthropologists admitted that they did not teach their students how to take notes. One undergraduate took no notes because he had no idea what to write (Sanjek 1990a). As to why they did not teach their students, some said it was too complex to even be teachable—that you only really learn by doing, that they had not been taught themselves (Jackson 2016). In fact, "Few anthropologists have even seen field notes before doing fieldwork" (Sanjek 1990a: 187). Margaret Mead was an exception who shared her field notes with her students. She wrote that she considered not doing so a wasteful system (Mead 1993 [1972]).

HOW TO TAKE JOTTINGS

It is good to start taking notes almost as soon as you enter the field. In fact, it has been suggested to take notes continuously when you are in the field. This will establish you as the person with the notebook. It will also avoid bringing attention to a particular event or person, which would be the case if you suddenly started writing furiously (Emerson, Fretz, and Shaw 2011).

Nuts and Bolts and Digital

You can take notes in a notebook. But what kind of notebook? A leather-covered notebook may mark you as someone who is affluent, while a formal notebook says you are an official. Something big stands out and is clumsy to carry. Each situation may call for a different type. At an elementary school, a notepad with bears, bunnies, or Disney characters will signal that you are sensitive to school-age children. A small waterproof notebook with waterproof pen is popular for those heading to the rainforest, and in a pinch, you can even write on a napkin or envelope! Many cell phones have a notes feature, and you can type and save your jottings there; you can type them on a small tablet; or you can even talk into a tiny digital recorder. Depending on the situation, typing on your cell phone may be less intrusive, but most anthropologists still choose a notebook for general use—it is best for drawing diagrams and symbols, for mapping, or for doing any illustrations (Jackson 2016: 2). If you are using a notebook, you will want to leave space for making tentative interpretations, comments, coding, and other notations, either on the spot or later when turning your jottings into field notes. Write on half the page or leave the facing page blank.

You Can't Record Everything

Jottings have to be selective. You can't record everything. Several things will be happening simultaneously, there will be different activities by different people, or someone may be talking to you at the same time you are trying to observe. So you have to make a choice and also be flexible. What you planned to observe may be less important than something unplanned. And how do you know what is important? Likely you won't know until the fieldwork has been completed—a reason for recording as much as you can. Follow Malinowski's advice to Wedgewood to produce a "chaotic account in which everything is written down as it is observed or told" (quoted in Lutkehaus 1990: 304).

Be Sensitive to People

You will want to be sensitive to people's moods and needs. People can be uncomfortable with jottings, so you need to know when to jot and when not to. When young Orthodox Jewish boys pointed and commented about my student's note taking, he learned that Orthodox Jews refrain from writing on the Sabbath. Even when you have established a routine you may be surprised by some reactions. Participants in a divorce case were accustomed to the anthropologist writing notes, but: "On one occasion when finishing up a debriefing . . . [the mediator] began to apply some eye make-up while I was finishing writing down some observations. She flashed me a mock disgusted look and said, 'Are you writing *this* down too!'" (Emerson, Fretz, and Shaw 2011: 39). At the other extreme, an anthropologist on an army post found that making jottings was the norm, and he blended in easily. However if he stopped writing "more than one relaxing moment," he says, "[he] was stopped by someone demanding that I write something down" (Killworth cited in Bernard 2011: 293).

When people ask what you are writing, how you frame it can be important. One anthropologist realized that saying he was studying the children's behavior (on the playground) led children to think he was recording bad behavior—because that was a term used by playground monitors—and caused children to shy away. When he changed his response to say he wanted to see how children played, he had better results (Emerson 2001: 229). Another strategy anthropologists use is to include members of the culture in their jotting activities. For example, if you are taking notes on a dance, ask what the dance is called or who the main dancer is, and so forth, and then write it down as they watch, or ask them if your spelling is correct while showing them the notepad. We spoke of the importance of openness when making jottings and how this can ease the acceptance of the anthropologist in the field. But we also spoke of the importance of being sensitive to people's needs, to making them comfortable. There may be times that warrant keeping your jotting more unobtrusive or hidden—when taking notes will not be tolerated or be disruptive. You may have to duck out and do jottings elsewhere. In any case, you need to jot notes as soon as possible, within minutes (DeWalt and DeWalt 2011).

There may also be times when you can't write things down, as when you are participating in a dance, playing in a band, or are involved in some other activity. There may be times it might be best not to record at the moment, when you are emotionally involved as a participant. In fact, some anthropologists would argue for not taking notes at all. Some feel that writing would "[dilute] the experiential insights and intuitions that immersion in another social world can provide" (Emerson, Fretz, and Shaw 2011:22). Others say that writing field notes interferes with the relationship with the other (Jackson 1990b). One more consideration is the anthropologist who might feel discomfort and transmit that to the subject (DeWalt and DeWalt 2011: 163). Circumstances will dictate which approach is the best.

ETHICS

You should not put identifying information of a sensitive nature in your jottings. We have already mentioned the importance of privacy for the safety of those you study. Also, who controls field notes has come under question in some instances. David Wilkins, in a personal account of fieldwork in central Australia, writes that his findings, including all his field notes, were considered under Aboriginal control. The council considered themselves the rightful owners of his raw data (1992).

If you contract with an agency, they may own the notes according to the agreement. Some universities have written rules that give the university right of access to all materials collected by members of the university. And notes can be subpoenaed. The DeWalts suggest to change the names of individuals or assign codes and destroy materials with original names (DeWalt and DeWalt 2011).

The introduction of technology into fieldwork brings with it its own ethical considerations. What is the ethics of posting photos and text to share on Instagram, Facebook, and other Internet sites? When will you be infringing on the privacy of the people you are studying? These are important considerations.

WHAT TO WRITE

Jottings are about fleeting moments. Notes taken at the moment have to be able to pull you back to that moment when you later write them up into field notes. And because you need to write jottings quickly, they need to conjure up an entire event from a few words. To aid in memory, anthropologists often use *mnemonic devices,* key symbols or short words or phrases of something unique that will jog their memory back to the event—"a bright green chair," "strong smell of incense," "squawking bird," "sudden downpour." These short phrases will not end up in the detailed field notes written later but will serve to bring back the moments. Sensory words, for instance, bring back the "feel" of the moment (Emerson, Fretz, and Shaw 2011: 32).

You may also jot down events of the day, food served at a festival, pieces of conversation, especially a phrase or short quote that seems important. Create sketches or maps of where people are located at a meeting or event, the locations of buildings or huts, what is sold in the market. All of these will be brief and may be chosen because you think you will forget (DeWalt and DeWalt 2011).

The new quickly becomes familiar and ceases to be noticed. This is why it is important to record first impressions as you encounter them—gestures, flavors, shouts and whispers, smells, people and their emotional and physical appearances, the environment (noises, colors, weather, tone), where things are and what they look like. What are others focusing on? What seems important to them that may not seem important to you? Cast a wide net early because when you start observing, you don't know what is going to turn out to be important. Rosaldo spent hours bored as his collaborators insisted on talking about place names with real emotion. Only later did he understand the names' significance as a key to how people thought about the past (Rosaldo 1993).

Make sure when you take jottings you differentiate between what you saw (objective) and how you interpreted what you saw (subjective). Be careful about imputing motive. What you saw is her eyes were red and swollen, what you interpreted is she probably had been crying for a long time. The first describes the scene, the second will need to be verified. Also just saying a person was angry will not be helpful. When writing it up later, you may not remember what made you write that. Instead, describe a person's gestures, words, and facial expressions. Of course you can make preliminary stabs at explanation as you record, but make sure you note these as such, knowing they may well turn out to be false. For example, the researcher who described the homeless as loitering on the street later discovered they were actually waiting in line for sleep tickets at the shelter (Emerson 2001: 133).

Describe the individuals' behaviors. Give the number of participants, their roles in the event (e.g., waiter, club president), status or hierarchy if that's relevant, and who is doing/saying what with whom. Following is a brief list of "jottings" dos and don'ts (Marti 2013):

> **Do:** Alice and Bob spent the entire hour playing Grand Theft Auto (a video game).

> **Don't:** Some people at the party were playing a video game while others talked and ate.

If you don't know names, use descriptive terms, but avoid judgments or stereotypes

> **Do:** baseball-cap man, little girl with ponytail

> **Don't:** funny looking person, sly lawyer, rude waitress

Only record what you actually saw/heard; don't make guesses. This means gossip, stories, or reported speech are OK, but they must be labeled as such.

> **Do:** Alice accused Bob of stealing Carl's lunch.

> **Don't:** Bob stole Carl's lunch.

Describe observed behavior in detail; don't use vague descriptions of mental states or attitudes.

> **Do:** B shouted at A and slammed the door on his way out.

> **Don't:** B got mad.

EMOTIONS

You may want to make jottings about how you feel and expand on these emotions later in a separate journal or diary, along with whatever else you write in your personal journal. Many have found that writing about frustrations and personal reactions in the field is cathartic and use the process as an emotional outlet (Sanjek 1990a: 27–29). Recalling one's feelings can also assist in reconstructing an event and interpreting the data, which will become part of your field notes. In addition to a diary or journal, field notes are also useful for "keep[ing] a grip on your sanity" (Jackson 2016: 11).

Jackson found that all the anthropologists she interviewed had strong feelings about their jottings. Some felt they were linked to their identity (2016), others that they made them "a member of the club," made them feel proud—"it's very gratifying seeing it all in one place," and made them feel productive. But negative feelings emerged as well: "they feel very inadequate. . . . Those notes reflect disappointments, frustrations, inadequacies. They reflect all I accomplished, but also all I didn't accomplish" (Jackson 2016: 48). Because of these feelings, many felt protective about their field notes—that they were private and not to be shared.

WRITING UP FIELD NOTES

While the topic is still undertaught in classrooms (Jackson 2016), a number of good sources have been published in recent years on writing field notes, as well as keeping other sorts of logs and records. Here, I will not go into detail on how to turn your jottings into field notes. A few words will suffice. Some say it is imperative to write up your field notes as soon as possible while you remember and can fill in the gaps. Margery Wolf recommends writing at once, because a year later your field notes look very different from the cards (jottings) on which the observations were recorded (1992). Your field notes are a fleshed-out version of your jottings and contain much more detail—important facts that will support your data. Others argue that you need to leave the field, that distance is important. Sanjek (1990a: 89–90) mentioned you may need some distance in the interpretation process. Lévi-Strauss wrote up his field notes in Paris after he left the field because he needed distance.

When writing up field notes from jottings, we are also pulling on what have been called "headnotes." These are the things we have "come to know without even knowing them" (DeWalt and DeWalt 2011: 172)—what is in your mind but has not been committed to paper (Sanjek 1990b: 93–94). We all use headnotes. As we write up field notes it becomes clear that much of what we remember we never wrote down, but these memories get incorporated into the final product. Ottenberg writes that headnotes change as we reassess what we remember and that we view it differently over time (cited in DeWalt and DeWalt 2011). In fact, some anthropologists rely mostly on headnotes and rarely write jottings (Emerson 2001).

As mentioned above, you may also want to have a separate diary or journal for expanding on your feelings from your jottings. Recalling your feelings will be useful when reconstructing an event and interpreting data (Stocking 1980).

SAVE THAT DATA

BACK IT UP! Fire, computer loss, even enemy action (Sanjek 1990a: 38) can destroy data. If you can, send data to a safe location while you are still in the field. These days this can be done digitally. But understand that technology will eventually go out of date: Where can you go nowadays to read those floppy disks? CDs also have a limited shelf life (Jackson 2016: 2), not to mention tapes and film. One solution is to mail copies of your field notes home or to upload them to an online storage site. However there is always the risk of your mail being misdirected or your online account being hacked, so your university IRB may require you to change or delete peoples' names or to remove other confidential information before sending.

Chapter Eight

Interviews

Here we look at the interviewing process, including structured and unstructured questions, how to avoid asking questions that make assumptions, and how to listen. The interviewee will, no doubt, be expecting a normal conversation. A successful outcome, however, requires an ethnographic interview, and the interviewer has to explain the difference. There also will be situations where even the ethnographic interview will not bring results. The anthropologist needs to know how to recognize when this is the case and what would be a better approach. All of these important aspects of interviewing will be considered here. Think of the following as guidelines, not rules—there are exceptions to almost every situation.

THE NUTS AND BOLTS

How many interviews should you conduct and for how long? It might be best to interview your interviewee several times, in short sessions. That way he/she will not tire and will be more likely to look forward to the next session. The first session will be an opportunity to get comfortable with each other and to let the interviewee know what is expected of him/her. The interviewee will likely want to please you and help you out. You will want to assure your interviewee there is no right answer and the person will not be judged on what they say. Each short session gives you the chance to demonstrate a nonjudgmental attitude and to build trust. Several short interviews also gives the interviewee time to reflect on the topics

67

covered and think about what he/she will want to say the next time. That having been said, if during a session your interviewee is "on a roll," you certainly do not want to cut the interview short.

You can use an audio recorder or take notes to record your interviews, depending on the situation. Make sure you ask permission to do either. You want your interviewee to feel comfortable during the interview, and in control. If your interviewee is uncomfortable with either, your memory will have to suffice. This is another reason for a short interview session. In these situations, you may need to duck immediately into the bathroom or run to your car where you can write down everything as you remember it. Be sure to always test any equipment you take with you before you arrive.

There will be questions you will want to ask, but never lose sight that your real goal is to discover what is important to your interviewee. You want your interviewee's story, and this can only be gained if you do not adhere rigidly to a set of questions. The sequence of questions and topics is not important; people do not remember in logical sequences. Flexibility will yield the best results. By being flexible, and a good listener, you can guide the interviewee through the maze of memories that will lead to the desired goal.

You might want to begin the interview by focusing on some of the areas you want covered. But remember, the best information comes when you let the interviewee take the lead. Try not to decide before the study what you will find. You will usually have some general ideas in mind (a hypothesis), and these will direct your questions. But listen well to your interviewee. Observe and record the nonverbal as well as the verbal responses. In the fieldwork situation, an interviewee often pulls the interviewer toward a topic the interviewee finds most interesting, or away from a topic she/he finds uncomfortable to talk about. Go with the topic that most interests your interviewee, but make sure you also get the information you need. Interviewing is a balancing act.

You will be negotiating your role during the interview, and this is crucial to a successful interview. You will want to move the relationship from "expert" (this is how you will probably be perceived) to student, with your interviewee as teacher. Here are some guidelines for making this transition:

- **Directed questions are best avoided:** Information can be gained by asking broad-based questions and speaking in general terms. Only ask specific and directed questions to fill in the gaps. Specific information often can be gained by asking for examples after a statement is made, or asking for elaboration of a point: for instance, asking, "Could you describe a typical day?" (See more on this below.)

- **Do not read off a list of questions at the interview:** This is intimidating. If you bring a list of topics to cover, show them to your interviewee but stress that you are not sure if these are the important things to cover. In general, it is best to bring out your list later, rather than at the beginning of the interview.

In some situations it might be useful to give your interviewee your questions in advance, for example, if an elderly person has trouble remembering (Anderson 2000). This would give the person time to reflect, but it would also give him/her time to invent. Again, each situation is different and you will use your judgment.

Ethics

It is important that you tell your interviewee that he/she will remain anonymous, that his/her identity will not be revealed. You should not use the person's real name. You may want to choose another name for your interviewee, or the two of you may want to pick the name together. Let the person know that any specific information that could be traced to an individual will be altered— place of work (such as the name of the restaurant and, if a chain, its location), her/his home address, place of origin if it is a small town or village, and other identifying information. It is also important to emphasize the value of the insights the interviewee will be adding to the general topic. For example, if your general topic is immigration, you might say that getting the "real" story of an immigrant will help dispel stereotypes and misconceptions many people hold about immigrants and the immigrant experience.

Finding a Neutral Topic

You need to anticipate how your questions will be interpreted. Especially important is to choose neutral topics for the start of the interviews. This is not easy. You may be surprised to find that what may appear to you to be a neutral question will be interpreted as anything but neutral. Some of these scenarios were covered in part 1. Imagine you are sitting in the living room of your interviewee, nibbling on the delicious cookies she has baked just for this occasion. Looking around the room for something neutral to comment on you see family photos framed and hanging on the wall. On the mantel is another framed picture, this one with candles in front of

it. Which do you choose to comment on? The wall hangings appear
to be neutral, but it might be best to wait before you comment on
the mantel photo. It could be the photo of a deceased relative and
part of a shrine. Both are in plain sight and both are thus public,
but just because something is public doesn't mean it is neutral.

Norma Mendoza-Denton found this out the hard way. Mendoza-Denton wanted to interview a member of the Nuestra Familia
gang. A meeting was arranged by a young high-school female gang
member who Norma had gotten close to in the course of her
research. The meeting took place in a laundromat where Manuel
(the gang member) was doing his laundry. After a faulty beginning,
the now flustered Mendoza-Denton was searching for a neutral
topic. She asked Manuel if he would talk about the meaning of his
tattoos, which were plainly in view. Immediately the young woman
grabbed Mendoza-Denton, saying, "We gotta go," and pulled her
out the door. She explained with a parable—"imagine you are going
to someone's house, it's their space, and you don't want to invite
yourself over, right? Like that, tattoos are stories, they are people's
personal stories and you have to be invited, to get to know them,
then they tell you" (2008: 113). Visible yes, but private and definitely not neutral.

Insider/Outsider

Many think that in an interview being the insider has advantages over the outsider, and in some ways this is true. The insider,
one who is a member of the same culture as the interviewee, has
the knowledge of cultural norms and practices and can fill in the
gaps and understand the context of what is being said. An insider
interviewing a family member has the advantage of knowing family history and dynamics and will be able to fill in what is left
unsaid. But there are disadvantages as well. Students who interviewed their mothers reported it was difficult to get them to sit
down long enough for an interview and then difficult to get them to
stay on topic. One mother wanted to talk while cooking or doing
dishes and kept her back to her daughter as she worked, or she
could only answer questions in between doing the laundry. The
interviewer often found her/himself being quizzed by the mother
about schoolwork or dates. One student, whose mother was an
executive and declared herself too busy for an interview, took her
mother's event calendar and penciled in a two-hour block. Another
student invited her mother out for coffee and an interview. But
even when a suitable place to interview has been found, one with

no distractions, and the interview has been brought around to the given topic, the insider is still not out of the woods.

When interviewing a family member, for example a son interviewing his mother or aunt, he is expected to already know the answers to many of the questions being asked. The son wants to hear again stories told to him as a child, in order to examine the utterances with the lens of the anthropologist. Mother and aunt are visibly annoyed. "Haven't you been listening to us?" they ask. "We told you about this many times before. Did you forget, or do you think it unimportant?" Here is where the outsider has the advantage. While the insider is expected to already know and is criticized for asking, for the outsider everything is patiently explained and, if asked, repeated again. The outsider is praised for wanting to know. The insider is criticized for having failed to listen.

Cultural Differences and Miscommunication

Charles Briggs (1984) warns about imposing the anthropologist's cultural norms on the interviewing process. This can lead to a clash of cultures where the expectations of each participant are at cross-purposes. He illustrates this blunder with his own experience interviewing Hispanics in a small village in the highlands of New Mexico. When he suggested to his "adopted" wood-carving family that they write a book on wood carving together, the couple were amenable to the idea. Briggs began by asking about the various steps in wood carving, but answers were not forthcoming. His "mother's" answer was usually *"ooo, pas, quien sabe?"* (ooo, well, who knows?) (23), and the most he could get out of his "father" were a very few words. Finally the couple suggested that Briggs carve alongside them. Now his questions, based on their interactions, with Briggs repeating what they said in the form of a question, brought forth information and explanations. The interviewing process had been reversed, with the interviewees directing the interview, and it worked. Briggs had learned how to communicate using another culture's norms.

Other anthropologists have chosen other solutions. The Peltos advise that the anthropologist choose a member of the culture who has experience with the cultural norms of the anthropologist, or choose a member of the culture who can be "trained" to understand anthropological interviewing methodology and to express his/her own cultural data in terms that conform to anthropological methodology (cited in Briggs 1984: 22). These are different approaches based on different experiences. No one way is right.

HOW TO INTERVIEW

The guidelines below are derived mainly from James Spradley's *The Ethnographic Interview* (2016 [1979]). The first interview sets the tone. In it, you will be developing a harmonious relationship between yourself and your interviewee. What is most important for your research is to find out what is most important for your interviewee. Following are some guidelines to accomplish that goal.

Develop Rapport

Developing a harmonious relationship between interviewer and interviewee involves building trust, getting comfortable, and enjoying the process. You can do this by being low-key, reassuring, courteous, attentive, and a good listener—the facilitator of the process of recollection. Look like a good listener—let the interviewee talk. Encourage talk with nods, smiles, eye contact, or leaning toward the interviewee. Make encouraging sounds of interest like "mmm" or short phrases such as "really?" to show you want the person to continue talking. Avoid fidgeting, drumming your fingers, or other actions that may make it appear you are anxious, impatient, or not listening. One way to develop rapport is by sharing experiences. If you have had similar experiences, share them. If you have not experienced the event, you can still share in it by saying, for example, "I would have been scared to death"; "I wouldn't have known what to do"; and so on. But remember, rapport can change; it is unpredictable. It can go from eagerness to reticence and back. Move away from uncomfortable topics (but note them for later). Let the interviewee set the pace. Allow for periods of silence.

James Spradley (2016 [1979]: 79–83) sets out four stages of rapport that are typical of the interviewing process. You will learn to recognize them.

1. **Apprehension:** Anxiety (Will I live up to the interviewer's expectations?) and suspicion are common. It is also common that people will want to please, to tell you what they think you want to hear, to want to represent themselves in the best light. Get the interviewee talking about anything. Then show interest and respond nonjudgmentally. Keep emphasizing the importance of each person's story, and show that you are not judging them.

2. **Exploration—sense of sharing:** Restate what the interviewee says for confirmation (use his/her key words or phrases).

Don't ask for the interviewee's motivations, ask for general use. Instead of asking directly "why did you do that?" say "when someone does such and such, what does it mean?" Put things in the hypothetical. Use "someone" instead of "you."

3. **Cooperation:** You are both participating in the interview as equals.

4. **Participation:** The interviewee accepts the role of teacher and begins to analyze his/her own experiences in order to get you to understand.

Friendly Conversation versus Ethnographic Interview

Your interviewee may expect this to be a friendly conversation, or they may expect a confrontational interview typical of the television reporting format. Your first step is to dispel any fear of confrontational-style interviewing. Next is to guide your interviewee from a friendly conversation to an ethnographic interview. We conduct conversations on a daily basis without ever analyzing the steps involved. As an ethnographer, you need to be aware of these steps in order to move your interviewee from conversation to ethnographic interview.

A friendly conversation lacks an explicit purpose; there is no agenda to cover. When your roommates come home from work, you wouldn't sit them down and say, "I want to ask you some questions about your work." In a friendly conversation you avoid repetition. Once something is said, it is not necessary to repeat it. In a friendly conversation each person takes turns talking. And both use abbreviations: referring to things known by both, with only partial information given. To your roommates returning from work, you are likely to say, "So, how did it go?"

An ethnographic interview is quite different. Here, there is an explicit purpose; both ethnographer and interviewee know where the conversation is supposed to go. The goal of the project, and how the interviewee's export knowledge will help to reach that goal, have been explained. And the interviewer repeatedly offers explanations to teach the interviewee how to become the teacher. Here there is no equal time for each person; you want the interviewee to do the talking while you mainly listen. Repetition is encouraged. Your role is to move the interviewee from friendly conversation to ethnographic interview.

Ethnographic Questions

A good way to begin interviewing is to go from the general to the specific. You can start with what Spradley calls *grand tour questions* (2016 [1979]: 86–88). You can ask the interviewee to describe everything he/she knows about a topic or event. Then to gain more understanding on a point, you can ask *guided tour questions,* such as "take me on a tour of a typical day" or "paint me a picture of what was happening." *Mini-tour questions* expand on the points that arise from guided tour questions. Finally, *example questions* are even more specific. Here you take a single act and ask for an example. *Experience questions* are like example questions in that they zero in on an event: "You probably had some interesting experiences in. . . . Could you describe them?" For *native language questions,* you ask about terms or phrases your interviewee used. In *hypothetical questions* you might ask: "If you were . . . , how would you say that, do that?" And for *verification questions:* "The last time we spoke . . ." Here, it is important to emphasize your ignorance and desire to learn—"I want to see if I got this right"— rather than sounding like you are testing your interviewee for the truth factor in a statement. A typical *contrast question* might be: "What is the difference between (term) and (term)?" All these questions are useful. Pick the ones that most fit your situation.

Avoid Leading Questions

From 1935 to 1939, Dorothea Lange was one of several photographers hired by the Resettlement Administration (RA) (later subsumed by the Farm Security Administration [FSA], which was housed in a government office in Washington DC). In 1964, Richard Doud conducted an oral history interview with Dorothea Lange for the Smithsonian Archives of American Art. It contains one of the best examples of "asking leading questions." This is what *not* to do in an interview:

> RICHARD K. DOUD: How did you feel about the organization of this thing? I'm not quite sure of what I'm trying to get you to say. For example, on your first trip to Washington, when you were first introduced to the people who were going to do this; perhaps a good deal of discussion about what was to be done, and how it was to be done, what were your reactions to the whole thing other than your initial excitement that something was to be done along the lines of photo-journalism perhaps? How did you feel about the actual organization of the work, being a part of Farm Security or Resettlement Administration at the time; working for a man [Roy Stryker] who wasn't a photographer, who was an economics professor, working in conjunction with other photographers whom you might or might not have known, or heard of?

DOROTHEA LANGE: You're describing something that I can see logically that you would expect to be that way. I mean, your good sense tells you that this situation must have led to that situation. You know, it wasn't like that at all.

RICHARD K. DOUD: I was afraid of that.

DOROTHEA LANGE: For me, it wasn't like that at all. You speak of organization, I didn't find any. You speak of work plans, I didn't find any. I didn't find any economics professor. I didn't find any of those things. I found a little office, tucked away, in a hot, muggy, early summer, where nobody especially knew exactly what he was going to do or how he was going to do it. And this is no criticism, because you walked into an atmosphere of a very special kind of freedom; anyone who tells you anything else, and dresses us up in official light is not truthful, because it wasn't that way. That freedom that there was, where you found your own way, without criticism from anyone, was special. That was germane to that project. That's the thing that is almost impossible to duplicate or find. Roy Stryker was a man with a hospitable mind, very hospitable. He's not organized, but he has a hospitable mind. He had an instinct for what's important. It's instinct. And he is a *colossal watchdog* for his people. If you were on the staff, you were one of his people, and he was a watchdog, and a good one. (Doud 1964)

Interviewing and Emotion

You need to be aware of two circumstances that may occur and how to handle them. As you gain rapport, the interviewee may want to make you her/his confidant. This can be because the interviewee said things he/she later regretted. Or, the person may have told you gossip, some of it malicious, such as talk about illegal activities and the like. Make a point of turning off the audio recorder, putting down your pen, and moving the interview away from these topics. If this does not work, just end the interview and, as politely as possible, leave. Another circumstance to be aware of is that memories may bring strong emotions. Emotional outbursts can occur. Here you want to stay with the interviewee until he/she is calm. If your interviewee becomes distraught and wants to turn the interview into a therapy session, let the person know immediately that although you are sympathetic you are not a trained psychologist. Offer to help him/her find a suitable clinic or therapist.

THE TRANSCRIPT

The next step will be to make a transcript of your interview(s). You will profit most by making transcripts after each interview session and reviewing them before the next interview takes place. A transcript is a written copy of the interview exactly as it took place. That means you include the pauses (. . .), sounds (mmmmm), "incorrect" grammar (do not change your transcript so that it is "proper" English), and words in a foreign language (with translation if you can). *Do not* edit your transcript. Include everything that was said, unless your interviewee asks you not to include something she/he told you, in which case you must respect the person's wishes. Your analysis will require a review of the entire interview. If you take out part of the interview, the analysis will be faulty. If you did not make an audio recording of the interview (the interviewee may not wish to be recorded), use your notes to write it up as close to the original as possible, and, just like with field notes, do the write-up as soon as you can while your memory is fresh.

Chapter Nine

Museums

When we speak of going into the field, that field can take many forms—a village, a military base, a homeless shelter, an archive, even a museum. The data we collect in the field include events (daily and special), conversations, interviews, and also material culture such as how people are sheltered and what they produce, distribute, and consume, from rice to the bowls it is served in, from fish to fishing nets, from mundane to ritual or sacred objects. For anthropologists, the museum is also a rich field site. In it are housed objects from the historical past, many of which are no longer found in villages of the present. But how these objects are displayed and the significance they are given can differ greatly, depending upon whether they are displayed in a Western mainstream museum or a native museum.

Years ago, there were Western museums that displayed indigenous objects according to Western perspectives, and there were no native museums where native objects could be displayed by members of the cultures that had produced them. Today, many mainstream museums in the Western world are more culturally sensitive. For example, the divide between what is considered art (Western) and craft (native) is no longer acceptable. Indigenous art is considered just that—art displayed as aesthetically beautiful and valuable. The periods of colonization that resulted in collections of native objects that were often obtained through force are acknowledged, deplored, and apologized for. But even as native artifacts are treated with respect, the meaning of these objects and their importance for the cultures that produced them is often lacking. How they were meant to be displayed, according to native views, is often quite different from the way they are displayed in Western museums, and their original purpose becomes lost.

MAINSTREAM AND NATIVE MUSEUMS (WESTERN VIEW)

Museum-going begins at an early age. Many can remember an elementary school outing to a local museum, often a natural history museum with objects on display—gems, dinosaur bones, and cultural artifacts such as beaded dresses, baskets, fishing nets, and spears. We come to the museum to look at interesting objects whose function and purpose will be explained. We come to be informed, to learn, from labels, videos, sound recordings, booklets, lectures, and interactive displays. And we come to museums to see rare objects and pieces of art of aesthetic beauty whose value is often measured by monetary worth, pieces displayed under glass or protected behind velvet ropes with guards posted in each room to assure nothing is touched, broken, or stolen. In art museums, the atmosphere is hushed, and viewing is almost an homage.

We are so used to thinking of museum exhibits from this Western perspective that we don't question how they are exhibited—we see them as natural. But what appears natural in a Western or mainstream museum is culturally constructed. There is much that influences the outcome of a museum exhibit, most of it hidden from sight. Michael Baxandall (1991) tells us that there are at least four participants involved in a museum exhibit and the role each plays is different, and often in conflict. We see the "native" object, but behind each object is the object's maker, often anonymous, working within the confines and values of his/her culture. Does the way the object is displayed reflect those cultural values? Or does it reflect the worldview of the curator? Is the curator following the directives of the museum board? Or the museum's funders? If it is a public museum, funded by the government, we would expect the exhibit to teach the values of the nation; if it is a private museum, the values of its founders. And then there is the Western viewer, trying to make sense of the exhibit, working within the confines of the cultural norms of Western museum-going, which is part of the viewer's own worldview and values.

Today, museum curators in mainstream museums are likely to consult with native members about which objects to display and how to display them. Cooperation can result in exhibits of value, but cooperation doesn't always result from these meetings, which can also be arenas of misunderstanding. James Clifford (1997) describes the meeting he observed at the Portland Art Museum in the late 1990s. Imagine a long table around which museum staff and native tribal elders meet—the latter invited to collaborate on an exhibit of Indian objects, blankets, baskets, and masks. The Western curators set the agenda. They expected that each object would be placed in the center of the table to be discussed—about how it should be exhibited and what needed to be printed on the label that described its importance and purpose. What transpired was not what they had expected. Each elder who was in some way connected to an object began to chant, to speak to the object and invoke its spirits. Each object had a story and each story was tied to a current injustice. The curators were given the message that they had a responsibility, when displaying an object, to right a cur- rent wrong—for example, the native grievance that their fishing rights were being curtailed. No dialogue took place around that table. In the end, the museum would not take up the challenge, arguing it was not the museum's role to politicize. The elders stood, thanked the curators, and left. The outcome of the encounter between native elders and museum staff reflected the unequal power of these two groups: the museum's agenda overrode the elders' wishes (Clifford 1997).

Several years after Clifford's experience at the Portland Art Museum, the National Museum of the American Indian (NAMI) joined the complex of Smithsonian museums. One of its special exhibits was titled *Our Peoples: Giving Voice to Our Histories*. On a wall at the entrance of this exhibit was mounted a large poster where one could read: "This museum rests on a foundation of 'con- sultation, collaboration, and co-operation with Natives.' It has shared the power museums usually keep. The place you stand in is the end product of that sharing, a process of giving voice" (Smith and Rosen 2011). This was a step toward correcting the inequali- ties played out in the Portland Art Museum years earlier, but there were questions and criticisms raised as well. The Smithsonian, as a national museum, was criticized for homogenizing Native Ameri- can peoples and for leaving out any reference to intertribal con- flicts. How influenced was the NAMI by government politics? How much voice did tribal leaders have and did this voice equal that of Smithsonian curators? These are questions that the anthropologist who uses museums as field sites needs to ask of the data collection. Whose voice(s) do we hear? Are there agendas being forced on the displays of objects? What is included and what is left out?

NATIVE MUSEUMS

Whereas the mainstream museum is a place that invites out-siders to learn about what may be unfamiliar to them, the tribal or indigenous museum is often a local museum for the local commu-nity, a place of gathering, emphasizing kinship ties and local owner-ship of objects. It is a method of communicating—storytelling—and an outside audience is not the main target audience (Clifford 1991).

The display of potlatch masks is a good example. Potlatch was an important gift-giving ceremony traditionally held by noble First Nations families of the Northwest Coast. The distribution of an abundance of food and gifts elevated the status of the giver and honored the recipients. The ceremonial dances involved elaborate costumes and carved masks. In 1884, the Canadian government banned potlatches, although the government was not able to elimi-nate them. It was not until 1951 that the ban was lifted (Kehoe 2003). If raided, members of First Nations groups holding an ille-gal potlatch could avoid imprisonment if they handed over the masks and other ceremonial objects. Many of these confiscated masks and objects ended up on display in Canadian museums. One group, the Kwakwaka'wakw people (formerly misnamed the Kwakiutl in some early ethnographies), were eventually able to negotiate the return of masks from the National Museum of Man on the condition that they would be displayed in a native-built museum (Olin 1983). The U'mista Cultural Center is the Kwak-waka'wakw First Nation museum and cultural education facility in Alert Bay, British Columbia, Canada. It was planned and built, and is now run, by tribal members to house potlatch artifacts that had been seized by the Canadian government at an illegal potlatch in 1921. *U'mista* means "the return of something important" (U'mista Cultural Society n.d.).

Whereas a mainstream museum would be likely to take a his-torical approach to the display of potlatch masks (while acknowl-edging White power) or an aesthetic one (as valuable pieces of art), this native museum would highlight the importance of these masks for the First Nations culture that produced them, by not only putting them on display but using them in ritual dances. For mainstream Western museums, the goal is to acquire, display, and preserve valuable pieces of art or artifacts considered important.

In a native museum the importance of these objects lies with their local meanings. Objects have family, community, and tribal ownership. Often museum labels do not explain the ceremonies in which masks are used, but rather they identify the families that own the masks. Chief Harry Assu of Cape Mudge Village explains the importance of the potlatch masks and other artifacts housed in the museum: "That's what the masks and other things mean to us: family ownership. Families lay claim to and have rights that are expressed in ownership of the objects, in stories and in dance" (Clifford 1991: 244). A gift shop worker, when asked about how tribal members felt about having artifacts returned, put it this way: "It's nice for them to have the artifacts nearby" (Clifford 1991: 230).

In the Canadian museum, protecting the masks behind glass display cases showed respect for an object considered valuable. In the native museum the masks are displayed in the open, in the places where nobles would sit at a potlatch. In the documentary "Box of Treasures," Gloria Cranmer Webster, curator of the U'mista museum, explains, "The objects in the Potlatch Collection have been arranged in this Big House space more or less in the order that they would appear in a potlatch. And they're not in cases. The feeling some of us had when the pieces were returned was that they'd been locked up for so long in a strange place that it seemed wrong to lock them up again" (Olin 1983).

THE POLITICS OF DISPLAY

Political battles are played out behind the scenes that determine how an exhibit is mounted or even if it reaches the public at all. These conflicts are rarely aired in public, but it is instructive when they are. An example of the politics of display is the Smithsonian's National Air and Space Museum (NASM) exhibit whose opening was planned to coincide with the 50th anniversary of the end of World War II. It was to feature the refurbished B-29 *Enola Guy*, the plane that dropped the atomic bomb on Hiroshima, Japan, but it would also include Japanese narratives and photographs of Japanese victims. Supporting the museum exhibit were a group of historians, but there were loud protests from the Air Force Association, American Legion, World War II veterans, and some members of Congress. The exhibit was cancelled, and a new one formed, dropping the references to the Japanese victims. This time, it brought the ire of the historians, who called for a national teach-in, and led to the resignation of Martin Harwit, director of the National Air and Space Museum. Tom Crouch, NASM curator, summed up the problem: "Do you want to do an exhibit to make veterans feel good, or do you want our visitors to think about the consequences of the atomic bombing of Japan? Frankly, I don't think we can do both" (Gallagher n.d.).

Not all national treasures are housed within museum walls, nor are they all objects. For instance, in Japan, a tea ceremony is considered a national treasure. So are the artisans who make the tea objects. The Ministry of Education chooses a list of artisans who are considered living national treasures.

Perhaps the advice given in the narrative mentioned above at the National Museum of the American Indian would well serve the anthropologist's encounter with museum data collections—"So, view what's offered with respect but also skepticism. Explore this gallery. Encounter it. Reflect on it. Argue with it" (Smith and Rosen 2011).

Chapter Ten

Archives

The historical anthropologist and the ethnohistorian study the past. Historical documents are their data, and archives their field site. These are not just dusty old documents but witnesses to once-living and breathing individuals. What separates the historian from the historical anthropologist is that the latter brings anthropological training to the research. The historical anthropologist seeks to understand the past through the eyes of those who lived it (Brettell 2000). He/she looks not just at the isolated documentary data but also at the culture that generated it. She/he interprets the data in the context of that culture and uses the knowledge of the culture to understand and test the validity of the data by identifying the culture's members and reconstructing cultural behavior. The historical record is also rife with distortions and gaps, and the ethnohistorian can also make use of these in reconstructing the past culture. For example, the bias of a census taker, who might distort data, is also evidence of prevailing attitudes: In counting families residing in a community, a 19th-century Mexican census taker left out members—the man's mistress and her family (Marti 1000). Thus, the ethnohistorical approach lends validity to the documents and turns problems and gaps into valuable evidence.

WHERE DO WE FIND ARCHIVES?

The National Archives and Records Administration (NARA) houses the most important documents generated by the United

States government. These documents, from the original Declaration of Independence to each veteran's service record, are available to the public. The University of Virginia Library and Project Gutenberg have available thousands of books, whose copyrights have expired, that can be downloaded in text or audio format. The Online Archive of California contains digitized collections from hundreds of California institutions, including historical societies, museums, and public and university libraries. And there are thousands of small, local archives such as the Echo Park Historical Society in Los Angeles, which houses oral and written histories, including one of residents of one street block almost a century ago (Harlow 1983).

Libraries on university campuses house special collections and archives. There are archives in museums and historical societies, and there are national, regional, and local archives. In fact, historical documents can be found almost anywhere. One just has to keep one's eyes and ears open. One enterprising young historian knocked on doors in the American South for documents related to slavery and was so successful she was able to write a PhD dissertation based on her findings in people's attics. Another researcher found some 19th-century postcards of markets being sold by antique book dealers from tables and blankets spread out on sidewalks outside the markets on Saturday afternoons in Mexico City.

Other examples of private collections are those managed by families, such as the archive started by General Reyes, minister of war under President Díaz, located in the Mexico City family home. And the private collection of 19th-century photographs was housed in a photography shop run by Sr. Victor Arauz who inherited it from his father. The former archive is open to the public, but to have access to the latter, one has to be introduced by a Mexican scholar. Many archives are digitizing their documentary material and making them available online (see below), but there is much more to be found on the Internet. I was able to locate photographs of old markets on Flickr and on several sites that sell old postcards.

WHAT IS A DOCUMENT?

The list is too long to include everything, but here is a sample of documents that can be found most anywhere—in archives, historical associations, a trunk in an attic, or online. They come in many formats: print, audiovisual, digital, electronic, and so forth. They can include the following: personal papers—such as letters, emails, diaries, photographs, daily planners, or notes; official records—such as census records, a driver's license, naturalization papers, and birth, death, and marriage certificates; school records—such as diplomas and transcripts; institutional records—such as an organizations' minutes of meetings, rules, financial records, internal memos, posters and brochures, and newsletters; media sources—such as newspapers, magazines, broadcasts, advertisements, pamphlets, handbooks, and even books. They can be documents that were meant to be used on a one-time basis, such as posters for events, theater tickets and programs, political leaflets and television ads, and bumper stickers; or they can be more permanent film and audio records, such as oral histories, newscasts, and/or films of events (wars, parades, speeches, marches, protests). They can also be photographs, from family snapshots to official portraits, postcards, photographs from war correspondents, photographs on official documents such as passports or IDs, government-sponsored photograph projects (such as WPA project that documented the dust bowl of the 1930s), or artistic photographs of American Indians (Edward S. Curtis) or natural wilderness (Ansel Adams).

Documentary collections are seldom complete. There are many reasons for gaps in the archives—some accidental and some intentional. Fires, earthquakes, floods, mold, mice, and revolutions can all damage or destroy documents. One example is Mexico. Disasters have destroyed materials for every period of Mexican history. Colonial Mexico is known for its duplicate (and triplicate) copies of official documents—originals were housed in the colony while one set was sent to Spain. Since fires and riots in 1624 and 1692 destroyed many official documents in the New World, scholars researching these years have to go Spain and consult the Archivo General de Indias in Seville. Poor-quality paper is another reason for gaps. An editorial in an 1895 Mexican newspaper complained that most factories produced such poor-quality paper that documents printed on it would not last. Intentional gaps include materials in the President Benito Juarez archive, which is under the control of his descendants. Anything that damaged Juarez's reputation has been scissored out, presumably by his father-in-law or other family members (Marti 1990).

But even events such as these can shed light on the past. For instance, many documents from the Porfiriato (the rule of Porfirio Díaz, 1876–1910) were damaged or destroyed by reusing the paper later on, during the 1910 Mexican Revolution. This is evidence of scarcity during that period of unrest—in this case scarcity of paper.

You might also find information not available to many at the time. As mentioned, my own research took place in the municipal archives of Guadalajara; I was looking for documents on markets and market vendors during the years 1870–1910. These included summaries of city council meetings published in the municipal gazettes—or rather, summaries of what were made public. I also discovered in the archives the minutes of meetings of secret sessions that were closed to the public and not to be released for 100 years. These documents shed much light on the behind-the-scenes workings of market administration. The public reason given for the removal of the administrator of markets was a conflict of interest: As administrator of markets he handled large sums of money while his position as senator gave him immunity from prosecution. In secret sessions, however, it was revealed that he had voted with the opposition party. In another secret session the matter of two market employees accused of falsifying documents was discussed. It was debated whether to investigate further, refer the matter to the police, or keep it quiet in order to avoid a scandal (Marti 1990).

DOING RESEARCH IN AN ARCHIVE: WHAT YOU NEED TO KNOW

The following is written from the perspective of a first-time student in the archives. Betty is standing in front of the glass doors to the Urban Archives at the California State University, Northridge. It is her first visit. She is carrying out an assignment on archival materials for her class in Anthropological Methodology. She can see there is activity in the room. Several large tables with chairs take up most of the central space. Each table has one or two people looking at documents. The doors are locked, and a sign instructs her to ring the bell. Betty pushes the button and a staff member quickly comes to the door. Curiously, she is not invited in. The staff member points to a row of lockers to one side of the door and tells Betty:

> You will need to store your personal belongings. We will give you a key for a locker. Put in the locker your backpack, pocketbook, briefcase, computer case, sweater, jacket, hat, or any loose article of clothing. No food or beverage (including water) is allowed in the archives. If you need to bring in research material it will need to be reviewed by a staff member and stamped before you sit down. Do not bring in ink pens or

mechanical pencils. We will give you pencils and paper for taking notes. You can bring in a computer and a digital camera,
which you can use without the flash. And to request materials,
you will need a current form of photo identification (such as a
student ID, or government-issued photo identification).

Betty takes the key and stores her things, including a sandwich
and soda she will eat later. She also turns off her cell phone as
directed and returns to the glass door. This time, when she presses
the bell, Betty is ushered into the reading room. The staff member
shows her how to request materials. They can only be consulted in
the reading room. She will need to fill out a registration form and
then a request form for each book or box of folders. If she requests
materials during the 30 minutes before closing, they will be available the following day.

Betty listens carefully and is then taken to a table where she
can work. She asks for help, which is readily given. What box
should she request? She has been handed a list of the topics and
materials kept in the archives—but which topic to choose? Her professor had talked about how knowledgeable the archivists are
about the collections and how helpful in matching researchers and
students to materials they would find interesting, and she finds
this to be the case. Two collections pique her interest. One collection that looks interesting is the audio files of interviews of the
first women in the International Longshore and Warehouse Union
(ILWU) to work on the docks. When moving goods on the waterfront meant using hooks and brawn, men occupied these positions;
women were hired as desk clerks and secretaries. But when the
waterfront was mechanized in the 1960s, hooks and brawn were
replaced with forklifts, and women were trained to use them to
move cargo around the port terminals. Their stories, the first
women to work the docks, were recorded on tape and reside in the
archives. What was it like for these women? Betty wondered. Were
they accepted by men or was there resistance to their presence?
How did they handle it; how did they feel, how did they present
themselves on the docks? Did they make themselves look feminine
by putting on makeup or did they try to appear masculine to convince others they could do a "man's job?"

Another collection that looks interesting contains Japanese
internment camp newsletters published in Japanese and English
from nine different internment camps. These newsletters documented camp activities and gave insight into day-to-day life for the
Japanese interned there. It is a hard choice, but Betty decides to go
with the newsletters. She requests a box of newsletters from the

archive's collection of Japanese-American Relocation Center Newspapers and waits.

When the staff member brings the box she instructs Betty in its use. The procedures are straightforward:

> Only one box or book will be brought at a time. When you finish with the box or book, ask the staff member to remove it and replace it with the next requested item. It is very important to keep all documents and folders in the exact order in the box. Only remove one folder from the box at a time and insert an "out" card in its place to maintain the order. If the materials are not filed correctly in the box or are damaged, alert the Reading Room staff. Don't try to rearrange the materials yourself.
>
> The materials are primary sources and in most cases one of a kind, so the utmost care must be taken to keep them in good condition. They need to be kept flat on the table. Don't lean on them or write on, mark, fold, erase, or trace over them. If items require special handling, Reading Room staff will help you and provide specific instructions. Cotton gloves will be provided if needed.
>
> You can request that materials be duplicated (there will be a charge). Usually you will need to return the next day to pick up the photocopies. There are flags provided as place markers for this service. You can also request that materials be held for you for up to one week.
>
> When you leave the archives you may be asked to show the notes and materials to be inspected. Often there are surveillance cameras which are recording on video at all times.

When the box arrives, Betty delves in and is soon absorbed by the materials she finds. She makes notes with her pencil on the pad of paper provided by the archive—which news stories she wants to have photocopied to take home; the condition, type of paper, and any other aspects of the document that cannot be ascertained in a copy; and ideas and questions that occur to her as she reads. Her next step will be to analyze the documents.

When she returns home Betty goes online and is able to find more camp newsletters from Japanese internment camps that have been digitized. The University of Washington Library has digitized the *Camp Harmony News-Letters*, produced weekly in 1942 by Japanese Americans living in the camp. In these newsletters, readers are told that hot water is back in the laundry rooms and warned not to wash their cloths in the showers. They are also asked not to "borrow" eating utensils from the mess halls as they are running low and to also use toilet paper sparingly. There are announcements of births, marble tournaments (for 6- to 10-year-old boys) and a 9 P.M. curfew. Applications for work include dish-

washers, cooks, recreation leaders, and farmworkers for the East-
ern Oregon and Idaho sugar beet fields. There are several
editorials on the need for self-government: Internees are urged to
cooperate with officials in order to be involved in the running of the
camp rather than have the administration of the camp under the
control of the army. With this goal in mind, the newsletters warn
about complaining in letters written to the outside, complaints
that could end up in newspapers and be "misunderstood" (*Camp
Harmony News-Letters* 1997 [1942]). From these newsletters Betty
begins to piece together a picture of daily life.

From online materials, Betty finds descriptions of living quar-
ters being built at an internment camp that are widely contradic-
tory. These contradictions need to be explained. The American
Friends Service Committee (AFSC), a Quaker organization,
describes boxlike buildings being thrown together with only one
tiny window every 20 feet in the rear wall. The American Red Cross
(ARC) survey paints a picture of a sturdy building with screened
windows and doors. While the ARC calls them apartments, the
AFSC likens each tiny room to a rabbit hutch (Conrad 1942; Report
of the American Red Cross 1984 [1942].). With further research she
finds the federal charter that reveals that the American Red Cross
has a special relationship with the federal government whereby it
occasionally carries out activities delegated to it by the government
for which it receives government funding (American Red Cross
2007). Could this explain why the ARC is less likely to criticize government policies? On the other hand, the AFSC has a history of
criticizing government policies they consider unjust. A 1942 letter
to the executive secretary of the AFSC about the mistreatment of
Japanese Americans in West Coast internment camps strongly suggests that the AFSC become involved since it was known that the
only white men the Japanese Americans trusted were Quakers
(American Friends Service Committee 2014 [1942]).

CORROBORATING AND CONFLICTING EVIDENCE

As Betty's story shows, the more documents available for an
event, the clearer the picture becomes. Corroborating evidence
strengthens the case and gives a fuller picture, but conflicting evidence can shine a light as well.

According to census figures, 19th-century Guadalajara wit-
nessed a growth of French and American enclaves, an influx of for-

eign business, and economic disparity. Corroborating evidence can be found in letters. For example, one letter is from a foreign establishment interested in setting up a cookie factory and asking about what tax exemptions they could expect (Marti 2001). That there was a growing gap between the rich and the poor is also corroborated by a comparison of factory wages with the price of a meal in a high-class restaurant: A meal at the fancy Chinese Wong/Tong Restaurant cost the same amount as a factory worker's weekly salary. Two pastries at La Fama Italiana could be had for a worker's daily wage (Muria cited in Marti 2001).

Conflicting evidence can also give us a fuller picture of events. In the archives we also find evidence that laws may not result in desired behavior, as seen in government regulations of markets. For instance, the law required a standard for cleanliness for foods in the markets, but other documents show difficulties in enforcing this. Inspectors reported throwing out rotting vegetables, putrefied fish, and diseased meats. One newspaper editorial gave a hint as to why: It complained that there were just not enough food inspectors for the job (Marti 1994).

GUIDE FOR WORKING WITH DOCUMENTS

Many of the questions asked of a document are not easy to answer. Think of yourself as a detective piecing together an event from the past with a minimum of clues. Your analysis will involve your imagination as well as your analytical skills. One problem is that you are looking at the past through the lens of the present—using assumptions, values, and experiences of today to understand yesterday. We do this without examining these assumptions, values, and experiences. Try to put yourself in another era with another set of values and assumptions. It takes some practice, and there is always room for improvement.

The following questions can guide you in your analysis of a document. The goal is to gain insight and understanding of the past. Some of the questions are straightforward; they ask for factual information. Others require interpretation, which involves imagination. Not all these questions can be answered by the document you are examining. And you may think of questions that can be answered by the document that are not included in this list.

The questions below are derived mainly from two sources: Kishlansky et al. 1991 and Kishlansky 2003.

- Identify the type of document (a letter, an official form, a diary, a newspaper article, etc.).
- Where was the document produced?
- When was the document dated?
- Who was the document's author? What do you know of the author—class, race, gender? How could the author's identity influence the content of the document?
- Is the document contemporary or after the fact?
- Was the document meant to be public or private? (For example, is this a written law, which is public, or a letter sent to a specific person such as a son or daughter, or a diary or journal that is meant for the author's eyes only?)
- Is this a translation? (Meanings can change, especially if the translator is not fluent in the original language.)
- For whom was the document meant? Can you tell by the language? What knowledge does the author assume the audience has?
- For what purpose or motive was it written? Does it mean to convince by logic? Is it meant to appeal to emotions? To intimidate? To inform?
- What biases or assumptions could color the views of the author?
- How familiar was the author with the subject matter? Do you have information that the author either lacked or chose to ignore? Do you think it was done intentionally?
- How familiar was the author with the person/audience for whom the document was intended?
- What factual information is available from the document?
- What other information is it possible to glean from the document?
- What light can the document shed about the family members, society, the time period in which it was written, stereotypes held at the time, etc.?
- What can be "read between the lines"?
- How reliable or believable is the document (or parts of the document)? How credible is the information?
- Could the document have been tampered with?
- What questions were not answered by the document?
- Does the document point to difficulties and dead-endedness encountered during the research process?

- How do the assumptions, ideas, or values conveyed by the document differ from those of our times? How does this influence how we interpret the text?

- The historian is not neutral but brings his/her own background and experience to the interpretation of documents. It is said that "every man/woman is his/her own historian." What does the document mean to you?

I have found in every archive I have worked in that the staff are knowledgeable and extremely helpful. In fact, they are crucial to the archival endeavor. In the Guadalajara archive just mentioned, staff members knew the collections well. This was especially important since during the time I was doing research the archive collections were being reclassified, and retrieval of the documents I wanted depended on staff memories. This was to be repeated in archives on two continents. At the 42nd Street New York City Library, a researcher must fill out a form with the title and author of the books requested. When you became a "regular," the staff who were retrieving your books would often include additional books on your topic, books you might not have been aware of. I found the same helpfulness in the Paris National Library and in the Bancroft Archive at UC Berkeley. Archive staff are not just knowledgeable, they are extremely generous with their expertise and time.

Chapter Eleven

Photography as Anthropology

Photography plays a major role in anthropological fieldwork. Photographs are invaluable as historical documents and essential to anthropological fieldwork. Cameras are standard equipment in the field.

PHOTOGRAPHY AND THE CAMERA AS METHODOLOGY

Photographs can be more effective than descriptions; much can be gained from a close reading of a photograph, but it takes training to see what we are not accustomed to seeing. This is where the trained anthropologist excels. We live in a sanitized world, writes Susanne Kuehling, and thus "may not realize how important scent is to a culture" (2009: 14). She goes on to say that photography can be even more effective than a description in evoking scent and helping Westerners to understand its importance in everyday life in other cultures; scents such as smoke from cooking fires, coconut cream smeared on the skin, and the perfume of strongly scented flowers all float in the air and are an integral part of life lived in the tropics. A photograph can document that aspect of life. In a photograph of a dancer, Kuehling (2009: 14) brings our attention to the sweat on the dancer's skin and invites us to consider the strong scent that would exude from a combination of sweat and the dancer's floral decorations.

I can't think of one anthropologist who goes into the field without a camera. Yet methodology courses do not always address how to use the camera as an anthropological tool. In the field, it is important to know what you want to accomplish using the camera and then choose the anthropological method that helps you meet that goal. The camera can be your visual pen, recording data in the form of visual field notes. Or it can be used to illustrate the written record, or to corroborate it. It can also be a tool for collaboration and an aid for discovering the insider's worldview.

The camera as methodology has a long history. Gregory Bateson and Margaret Mead, who worked in Bali and New Guinea, wrote of introducing a new method, that of using cameras as "recording instruments, not as devices for illustrating our theses" (Bateson and Mead 1942: 49). With this new approach, one used a camera the same way one would take written notes, recording events and interactions as they occurred, to mimic direct observation. The usual approach at the time was to take photos of events to illustrate the interpretation you had already given to those events. But you don't have to choose between recording data observed or illustrating interpretations—both are useful approaches. Bateson and Mead also suggested three methods for using the camera as unobtrusively as possible: (1) Always wear a camera around your neck so people get used to it. (2) Photograph babies—the adults will forget they are being photographed too. (3) Use an angular viewfinder so it appears you are pointing elsewhere (1942: 49). Today, these raise ethical questions about filming unawares. There is a difference between trying to be unobtrusive and not informing people that you are taking their picture.

Treating the subject as collaborator is the preferred approach. Changes in technology, with smaller digital cameras and disposable cameras, allow for even more collaboration than was previously possible, when cameras were large, bulky, and expensive.

THE SUBJECT AS COLLABORATOR

Photographs taken by the anthropologist can be an important method in anthropological fieldwork when the anthropologist collaborates with members of the society. They can serve as a window to the insider perspective, often with surprising results.

John Collier used a method he termed "photo interviewing." He assumed dance to be an integral and important aspect of Puebloan religious life; after all, the Deer Dance was *the* key event in the summer's festival. However, when Collier interviewed collaborators about its importance, showing them photographs of the dance, he was surprised to hear them say "we do this to please the white people" (Collier 1988: 90).

Photojournalist student Akiko Arita used photography as methodology on a Navajo reservation and the result was an excellent thesis of the Navajo belief system and culture from the Navajo point of view. Her method was to take photos of daily life and then ask for Navajo participation in the selection of photos that best represented the most important aspects of Navajo culture. Members of the tribe sat around a large table, stacks of photos spread out across the tabletop, pulling out those considered important and discussing why. She was often surprised when many chose a photo of something she had thought inconsequential or trivial, while ignoring photos of what she had considered important events. She had expected family to be important, and it was. That women's roles were also considered important was a surprise. She told me that without the native perspectives on photographs, she would not have been able to uncover the fundamental nature of native culture (Arita 1994).

Fadwa El Guindi was also surprised by insider interpretations of photographs. El Guindi used a methodology she called "slide-elicitation technique." When interviewing a native she would include slides (nowadays photographs or digital images would be used instead of slides) of the events or objects about which they were speaking. It served as a tool to cross-check the data she had already collected, as well as a method for drawing out additional information. As part of her research she frequented the village cemetery where she took pictures of the cemetery shrine. She had watched caretakers pound the dirt over graves using two stones they then placed on top of the shrine. When she showed slides of the shrine—with the two stones atop—she was surprised to discover that those stones were not considered utilitarian objects conveniently placed. She was unaware that they had any important meaning or status, but by using this method she was able to learn that, in fact, the stones were sacred (El Guindi 2000).

Another method is to provide members of the community with cameras and ask them to take pictures of what they consider to be important. Photographs taken from an insider's perspective, it is felt, will yield insights into cultural behavior and beliefs. This can be extremely useful, but, as the following illustrates, there are pitfalls as well.

Georgina Drew (2009) calls her approach "participatory photojournalism." With this method, three children, three school teachers, and three activists in the village of Mehdiganj, India, were supplied with cameras (35mm, digital, and disposable), film, and lessons in taking photographs. They lived in an area of water shortage and were in constant conflict with a local Coca-Cola bottling plant over this scarce resource. Outsiders had covered the story, but this project sought to allow insiders the opportunity of documenting their own lives and struggles. A magazine specializing in documentary stories agreed to publish the results.

Several weeks later Drew returned to the village to develop the film and discuss the photographs with the participants. What surfaced was the first of several unexpected problems. A power hierarchy had dictated the distribution of cameras. The 35mm cameras were given to the school teachers, children were given disposable cameras, and the digital camera was kept by the activists. Not surprisingly, children took pictures of other children and activists took pictures of protests against Coca-Cola. Teachers took aesthetically beautiful pictures of women and men planting rice and carrying water. There was unexpected camera use as well. Cameras appeared to have been more widely used by people unknown to the anthropologist (when the photographer appeared in the picture, this was a clue!). They had been lent out to friends and relatives for purposes other than the project. One activist used the camera to document his vacation trip. One of the most disappointing outcomes was the final result.

The magazine chose the aesthetically pleasing photos, which gave the impression that villagers were passive rather than assertive and angered the movement members who had photographed village protests and whose goal had been to give voice to their plight (Drew 2009).

PHOTOGRAPHS AS HISTORICAL DOCUMENTS

When I did research on Mexican markets and street vendors during the Porfiriato, contemporary photographs served several purposes. I used them to corroborate documentary evidence, to provide information not obtainable from the written texts, and to fill in gaps in the historical record.

I was fortunate to be introduced to Sr. Victor Arauz who had inherited a large collection of historical photographs from his father. One of the turn-of-the-20th-century photographs I bought from him documents the Guadalajara Mercado Alcalde (see photo 1). It shows the entire side of the Mercado Alcalde blocked by vendors who laid out their merchandise on the ground. Lists of goods sold by vendors that I found in the archives corroborate the evidence from these photographs that the vendors were selling dolls, blankets, and pottery. What the photograph below also reveals, which is not possible to ascertain from the documents, is that the women vendors were ethnically Indian. Documents list the names of vendors, but since Indians carried Spanish names, they are indistinguishable from mestizo or Spanish vendors. From photographs we can see the women dressed in Indian clothing wearing typical Indian shawls or *rebozos*.

From other photographs I bought, one can trace the routes of Guadalajara water vendors (*aguadores*). The first photograph shows water vendors at a public fountain. One vendor fills an earthenware pot with water from the fountain, while two other vendors wait at the carts they will push, lifting the heavy carts by their wooden handles and propelling them on their one wheel, down the street of Guadalajara, each cart with its four large clay pots. Another vendor uses a donkey to carry the burden. The animal waits patiently, four pots strapped to the frame on its back (see photo 2). In another photograph, the vendor is pushing the same type of crude frame for carrying large jugs of water like the ones in the previous photograph. He is crossing one of the main thoroughfares in Guadalajara (see photo 3). A fourth photograph depicts a water vendor who has stopped his cart to sell water at the cross-section of two streets, which we may infer is a busy intersection given the trolley tracks. His customer is a small boy who will carry the water away in two smaller jugs balanced across his small shoulders (see photo 4). Yet another vendor

1. Women selling pottery, blankets, and dolls outside the Alcalde Market, Guadalajara, Mexico, circa 1898–1902.

sells smaller quantities of water from scooped out gourds balanced by a stick across his shoulder. He will sell it by using the metal cupful that he holds in his hand (see photo 5).

2. Water vendors filling containers in a square with a public fountain, Guadalajara, Mexico, circa 1900.

3. Water vendor pushing cart with large jugs of water across a main thoroughfare, Guadalajara, Mexico, circa 1900.

4. Water vendor selling at street corner to small boy, Guadalajara, Mexico, circa 1900.

5. Vendor sells water by metal cupful from gourds balanced by a stick across his shoulder, Guadalajara, Mexico, circa 1900.

Chapter Twelve

Digital Culture

Imagine yourself suddenly set down alone on a tropical beach close to an island village. Spread out before you on a gorgeous blue sea is an archipelago of islands and continents. While the boat that has brought you to this place sails away, you realize you are alone and have nothing to do but begin your ethnographic journey. You have no previous experience in conducting fieldwork in this environment; there is little to guide you and no one to help you. Thus began my two-year field study in Second Life. (Boellstorff 2009: 1)

Tom Boellstorff parodies Malinowski's oft quoted paragraph from *Argonauts of the Western Pacific* (which I quoted earlier in chapter 3) and likens his first forays into the online virtual world of Second Life as akin to Malinowski's first forays into the Trobriand Island village in Melanesia, with the same trepidation and the same lack of guidance.

DIGITAL/VIRTUAL ANTHROPOLOGY

Digital anthropology and virtual anthropology are terms that have often been used interchangeably, although the term "digital anthropology" may be gaining more use since it spreads a wider net to include the interrelationship between people and technology, looking at, for example, how people use technology as a tool or how technology creates community. The term "virtual anthropology" implies that ethnographic methods used in the physical world are extended to virtual worlds. This perspective has been criticized for treating the virtual community as an independent entity and emphasizing a dichotomy between online/offline and virtual/real communities that many would argue does not exist since individuals move frequently between the two.

Participant-observation traditionally took place in a physical place—the village square or a corporate office. Now anthropologists apply this methodology to virtual places, such as chat rooms, games, or social networking sites, replacing actual participant-observation with virtual participant-observation, because that is where people frequently are. Adam Fish writes that in his study on global video culture he may spend as much time interacting with people on Twitter or Facebook as he does sitting in on office meetings. The founder of the firm he was studying told him about this lack of physical place— "the key problem is that we do not have a 'site' . . . you can come to NYC but half the days there is almost no one here. Potentially a better approach is to have you do a 'virtual' site" (Fish 2011:17).

Most anthropologists would agree that digital or virtual anthropology is not a method. Rather, it involves applying traditional anthropological methodology, such as participant-observation, to new contexts online (chat rooms, blogs, online games, etc.) in a new global reality where communities are no longer only located in a physical place but are made up of people dispersed around the world. Anthropologists have always looked at community formation. They now include communities online. Anthropology is uniquely suited to study sociocultural online communities since the Internet itself is a cultural product and everything on it is culturally constructed (Wilson and Peterson 2002).

Online communities would include members of organizations that have worldwide membership, such as a community of fans who felt alone until they joined up with others. Or citizens of countries who have emigrated but who maintain their national identity through websites, such as Trinis who *lime out* (hang out) in a virtual place while they are far away from the real place, Trinidad (Bird and Barber 2007). There are also "imagined communities," whose members share a sense of community even if there is no longer a physical place (Anderson 1983), for example Assyrians who trace their heritage to ancient Assyria, a kingdom that existed around the 25th century B.C. in what is today northern Iraq (Bird and Barber 2007).

Many of the questions anthropologists are addressing are also not new: They are just being directed to a new arena—the Internet. There are questions about power—who has access to virtual technology, and are gender, race, and class factors? Questions about equality—can the Internet really be viewed as a utopia where anyone can construct an identity, thus creating an egalitarian space? Commentators in the media have pointed out that tech innovators in places like Silicon Valley are designing technology for urban elites, like themselves, who are often young, white, male, and technically savvy, and they are designing products too expensive for many, with knowledge to use these products not readily available to the poor (Wilson and Peterson 2002). Another question focuses on isolation versus connection—is the Internet alienating (the stereotype of a teenager alone in his parents' basement staring at a computer screen) or does it open a social window, for example, for the disabled and others who have difficulty with mobility or for mothers of small children who spend most of their time at home?

THE INTERRELATIONSHIP BETWEEN PEOPLE AND TECHNOLOGY

Technological advances create new forms of activity, attracting participants and creating newer field sites for anthropological research: such as television viewing, virtual worlds, or virtual games.

How Consumers Use Technology

Corporations hire anthropologists to study how consumers use technology to purchase goods and services. Companies need to sell goods: they need to know what people want. Intel Labs hired anthropologist Genevieve Bell to find out how customers interact with technology. How could Intel change, modify, or create technology that did what customers wanted? By using interviewing methodology, Director of User Experience Bell and her team of 100 researchers found that in China, parents saw computers as interfering with their children's schoolwork. So Intel developed a computer that allowed parents to block online games when children were doing homework. Participant-observation revealed that people regularly ignored their car's embedded technology and used the portable devices they carried with them instead. This led Intel to partner with an automobile manufacturer to develop a device that allowed customers to sync up their portable devices with their car's technology (Singer 2014).

Television Viewing

Early studies focused on the interrelationship between television and viewers. For instance, Lila Abu-Lughod (1997) studied the significance of television in the lives of Egyptian women. Using the method of participant-observation, she participated with village women as they watched a popular Egyptian soap opera, *Mothers in the House of Love,* and observed their responses in order to understand meanings in their lives. The author cautions against assuming that because they belong to the same nation, all Egyptians share the same cultural norms. The television program was written by a woman whose social and economic class, education, professional status, and urban living environment were vastly different from that of the peasant viewers in Upper Egypt who watched the episodes in their rural village.

The television writer's agenda was to push for women's power and equality. In her television scripts she portrayed older middle- and upper-class urban Egyptian women who had the chance for remarriage based on love, that is, the chance for a relationship of companionship. This message of women's emancipation struck a moral core among women in the rural village whose experiences were of arranged marriages and for whom remarriage was considered improper rather than liberating. A typical response was "we say when a girl is past thirty she won't marry. . . . It is shameful. If a woman over thirty does marry, she'll do it quietly, far away, without a wedding celebration" (Abu-Lughod 1997:27).

Online Virtual Worlds and Gamers

When television viewing, especially in the Western world, gave way to online gaming, anthropologists began to focus on this new arena. As more people divide their time between "real" and "virtual" worlds, anthropologists have also expanded their research to include online sites—after all, this is where people are—again using traditional anthropological methodology, asking the questions anthropologists ask.

Bonnie Nardi used as her field site World of Warcraft, an online role-playing game that several million people subscribe to, many playing in teams or large "raids" with other online players to explore or battle, group activities that can last for hours at a time. She wrote that she approached her online field site as she would an off-line field site, using the same methodologies, such as interviewing, both online and face-to-face. "I initiated the research with a desire to satisfy a deeply felt urge of the cultural anthropologist— to journey to a foreign land, and experience the strangeness of a new culture, to find out what the natives are doing and what they think about what they are doing" (Nardi 2010: 27).

For his master's thesis on World of Warcraft, Matthew Halpern took on the role of a warlock. The introduction to his thesis gives a sense of the anthropologist in the field:

> Hello, my name is Rannis and I am a level 85 Destruction War-
> lock. I have fought in the Sunken Temple, deep within the
> Swamp of Sorrows. I have stormed the Black Temple and wit-
> nessed first-hand the defeat of its master; Illidan Stormrage.
> Since my time in this world, I bore witness to the rise of the
> Lich King in the north and the Cataclysm that struck the lands
> of Kalimdor when the dragon aspect Deathwing the Destroyer
> awoke. I have seen much, yet nothing, for I am merely the ava-
> tar for which this player navigates through the lands of Aze-
> roth. Welcome to the World of Warcraft. (Halpern 2013: 1)

In addition to participant-observation, Halpern used anthropological methods of in-game and in-person interviewing (the latter at
game conventions).

In Second Life, often described as an online world rather than
an online game, you can attend classes and hear lectures, buy land
and build a home, and go to concerts, bars, and sex clubs. Although
other virtual worlds have appeared since its inception, as of 2014
Second Life still drew over one million users. Anthropologist Tom
Boellstorff established himself in Second Life in a home-office
called "Ethnographia" as an anthropologist doing fieldwork. Over a
two-year period of time he conducted research using traditional
anthropological methods including participant-observation, interviewing, and archival research. He focused on traditional areas of
study in anthropology, including place, social relationships, gender,
race, economics, and politics, and concluded that continuities
between the virtual and physical worlds are more significant than
their novel differences (Boellstorff 2008).

HOW THE MEDIUM SHAPES THE MESSAGE

Anthropologists also look at *how* people communicate using
technology. For instance, Professor Ilana Gershon asked her class,
"What counts as a bad breakup?" What she learned—and subse-
quently published in a book, *The Breakup 2.0: Disconnecting Over
New Media* (2012)—was not only about breakups through social
media and technology but about how the use of technology was
changing cultural norms.

Gershon looked at the relationship between the medium and
the message—how the medium shapes the message. What does the
medium (whether one uses texting, emailing, calling, posting on
Facebook, etc.) say about the message (in this case, ending a relationship), and what is the appropriate medium to use for the mes-

sage being conveyed? She found that while individuals have definite ideas about the appropriateness of the medium to use for a message, there is no real consensus, which can lead to misunderstandings.

There were multiple examples of misunderstandings of the appropriateness of what media to use for the message "I am breaking up with you" among students. Some said it was not a breakup until it was announced on Facebook or your status was changed (for example to single), and that should be done right away. Others said it was polite to tell your social network first because close friends would want to talk with you by phone before it was announced on Facebook. One student and her boyfriend had a joking relationship they conducted by texting. But when her boyfriend chose to break up with her in a text message, she found this inappropriate; texting is for joking and casual conversation, not for serious matters. In fact, at first she thought he was still joking *because* he was texting. Texting a breakup was bad behavior in her eyes, and she never spoke with him again (Gershon 2012).

Generational differences can also influence how one views the medium and the message. People from older generations tend to use emails to communicate for casual matters and still rely on letters for formal and/or serious matters. But younger people are more likely to use texting for casual communication and view email as the formal medium used to communicate with parents or teachers.

ONLINE RESOURCES

The Internet hosts many resources for the student and professional anthropologist. One American Anthropological Association (AAA) site of particular interest is DANG, the Digital Anthropology Group. A search of the Internet will provide numerous other blogs addressing topics of interest to anthropologists, and new ones are popping up all the time.

A caveat about online fieldwork: The DeWalts (2011) caution that there is a temptation while doing online research to forgo taking jottings and field notes since much of what you are observing is already recorded online. They would argue that it is still important to jot down your own descriptions of what is happening, including your role and your responses to the field site. Because it is so easy to record online activities, you may end up with a lot of detailed data, and field notes become especially important as a way to keep track of relevant or interesting occurrences or observations.

Chapter Thirteen

Autoethnography

Rosalie Wax recollects that

> as a university student and a researcher, I was not yet ready to accept myself as a total person, and this limited my perspective and my understanding. Those of us who instruct future field workers should encourage them to understand and value their full range of being, because only then can they cope intelligently with the range of experience they will encounter in the field. (Wax 1986: 148 cited in Bernard 2011: 281)

What Wax describes is often called the reflexive approach. It is an ongoing process of assessing one's personal and emotional barometer in fieldwork, of considering how one's own feelings, biases, and life experiences impact one's fieldwork. Recently, the trend for the anthropologist to insert him or herself into fieldwork has gained credence and now is its own subdiscipline and methodology known as *autoethnography*. After all, the fieldworker is neither a neutral nor an unaffected observer. Our personality and life experiences have a bearing on fieldwork—on the choice of site and topic, on how the data are collected and interpreted, on the choice of which individuals in the community to interview and/or observe, and on how those individuals react to us. Gender, ethnicity, sexuality, class, and other characteristics, as well as our emotional state and life experiences, affect—in a personal way—our fieldwork experience, the data we collect, and how we interpret that data.

Advocates of autoethnography also remind us that the fieldworker is not invisible to the population under study. The fieldworker influences the fieldwork situation, and the community also has an influence on the researcher. Both interact with one another in an ongoing relationship. Fieldwork experiences change the researcher, which in turn also affects the fieldwork. It is important to be aware of these factors and to be introspective. These insights are being incorporated into written ethnographies and are considered important elements in the final published work of any descriptions of cultural behavior or generalizations about cultural values.

It might be more accurate to say that reflexivity is being "rediscovered" because reflexivity in anthropology is not new. From Malinowski's famous introduction in *Argonauts of the Western Pacific* (2013 [1922], see chapter 3 pages 19–20 this volume) on, early anthropologists have noted the importance of looking inward. Malinowski argues that the emotions of the fieldworker can lead to greater understanding and thus are integral for the methodological approach of participant-observation. E. E. Evans-Pritchard wrote in 1937 that the researcher is changed in the field. Witchcraft—his area of study—permeated all conversations and actions in the daily lives of the Azande: "If one must act as though one believed, one ends in believing, or half-believing as one acts" (quoted in Emerson 2001: 246).

Gillian Richards-Greaves was drawn to Guyana, her field site, because it was the place where she grew up. But she found that it was not until she could move beyond her own prejudices that she could effectively do fieldwork in her place of origin. Richards-Greaves left Guyana when she was 17 years old and only returned 20 years later to conduct her dissertation research. She expected to be viewed as an insider, easing her entrance into the field and her fieldwork, but she found that this was anything but the case. Brought up as a Christian, she had to constantly overcome native suspicions that she would view native religious rituals as sinful, even though the focus of her PhD dissertation was *Kweh-Kweh,* a native ritual. Elders wondered how much she would know of the rituals, since she was really just "a little girl" when she left. But the greatest obstacle was her own prejudice: She could not view herself as a "proper" Guyanan woman. She refused to take part in conversations that urged women to "submit to their husbands" and "please their man," conversations that dominated daily discourse. Rather than listen to the women, she found herself detaching herself from them. It was only when she was able to move beyond her prejudice and stop rationalizing her behavior to the women, and really listen to them (including their criticisms of her own behavior), that she began to hear what was important to them (Richards-Greaves 2013).

Your emotions affect your relationship with people and the way you interact with them, which in turn affects the research. Anthropologist Annelou Ypeij (1998) writes about how the growing violence in Lima, Peru, changed the relationship she had with her collaborators, which in turn influenced how she interpreted the data. As grassroots organizations in Lima began to be infiltrated by members of a Peruvian revolutionary group, the grassroots organizers became suspicious of one another and of Ypeij, the anthropologist working in their midst. Some suspected Ypeij of being a police spy and distanced themselves from her. And Ypeij distanced herself from them because she was afraid that her presence would jeopardize the women organizers.

This shift in her relationship with the organizers also caused a shift in the way she interpreted the data. As she distanced herself from the women she was studying, she began to see them as one category and thus noticed their similarities, whereas when she originally had close emotional relationships with the women she saw them as individuals and mostly noticed individual differences.

It was only later, when she had left the field, that she became fully aware of her treatment of the data and also of her emotions, especially her fear. Because of the emotionally charged environment, it was difficult to acknowledge her own emotions and continue to function as an anthropologist while she was in the field. She writes that if she had acknowledged those emotions then, she would have fled (Ypeij 1998).

There are no large-scale studies on how anthropologists change in the field, but Jackson has interviewed several (2016). Like Ypeij, some said in the field they were so focused on the moment it was not until later, after they had left the field and were rereading their field notes, that they became aware of how they had changed. One anthropologist Jackson interviewed felt that "because she had become 'like a different person,'" she read her field notes "with a new eye. They are things that I wrote, that I did create, and now I have a different relationship [to them]" (Jackson 2016: 49).

Closer to home, students in my anthropological methodology class were asked to do fieldwork for one semester in a large western coastal city in the United States, choosing a community of immigrants as their field site. Students of immigrant families were not allowed to study their own community, so they all entered the field as outsiders. Their last written assignment was to be reflexive—looking back on the semester's research. Students wrote of how their own personality and life experiences affected their fieldwork and how that might have colored what they saw, or brought them to greater understanding of themselves. I will let these insightful student writings speak for themselves.

It comes through clearly that one cannot keep out emotions, nor should one. A student writes:

> It's hard not to let your own biases and the subliminal messages you've been brought up with affect your objective research on a culture. I tried to keep my emotions under control as my views and perspectives changed as I got to know the enclave better but now that I am writing an autoethnography I know that this is impossible.

My students wrote about their trepidation entering the field for the first time, then not only overcoming these fears, but regretting when it was time to leave. Overcoming fears often meant recognizing that the students themselves had to change:

> I decided to interact with the people in the store, rather than fear the stares of what I perceived to be "new person judgment." . . . I went from feeling like an outsider to feeling like a member of the family in a matter of a few short weeks . . . I learned something about them every day and I was given the pleasure of letting them learn a little about me and my culture. By engaging with them on a personal level I was easily let in which made them more inclined to share with me on a deeper level. [She adds,] I was very nervous wandering around. No one would talk to me, and I got the feeling as if I was intruding . . . but I got past my own insecurities and . . . my inability to speak to people. I was able to step outside of my comfort zone, and I am very proud of the fact that I was able to do that.

In the end, she expressed her desire to get to know the people in Little Cambodia better and "really discover the missing pieces. A semester is just not enough time to really get to know a group."

Another student tells us:

> From my very first meeting with the Tongan high school students I remember the fear that was with me the entire time I drove my car [to the site] . . . I kept thinking to myself, "Will I be able to get along with them?" "Will I stand out from the rest of them?" "How will I be able to talk to them?" I can remember hearing my heart pounding in my chest as I parked my car and walked towards the high school. . . . My hands were gripped tightly together in the pocket of my hoodie as I waited for school to finish and for the rest of the students to gather in the room. [The next trip to the high school was very different.] I arrived at the school this time and it already felt different. I

parked my car in the parking lot and walked towards the school. The sun was shining as my arms swayed back and forth. I was greeted with the girls shouting my name as they ran up to me.

Students also spoke of how their own background aided them in unexpected ways. Over time the Tongan girls came to regard this student as a role model, which she bases on her ability to use her own experiences to help students understand what was happening to them.

> With my experience I was able to relate with the girls the pressure that they feel coming from all directions . . . from their parents, friends, and from academics. I was able give the girls comfort . . . I was able to reassure them that it was okay for them to feel as if sometimes there is too much pressure for them to perform to please certain people. I gained their trust and they opened up . . . in ways that I never thought [of] before. I became almost like an unofficial older sister to some of the girls.

Students also wrote about how fieldwork changed them. One student wrote, "By getting to know them I have gotten to know myself and have grown in doing so." Another said, "When I visited the ethnic enclave for the first time I saw it with different eyes, and I saw many details I had never seen before. A different door opened up to me . . . [I became] more tolerant and patient . . . so [this] is a very powerful gift." And a third found that "through these encounters, one thing I have learned to be is a bit more forgiving of people who initially come across rude."

My students ultimately reported positive outcomes—fears overcome, insights gained, and welcoming community members. Many anthropologists write of similar outcomes. Anderson spent 30 years traveling the world and almost all of these field trips resulted in close relationships and insightful ethnographies. But there will be exceptions. One has to know when it is time to just walk away. Anderson realized, "despite my affection for Morocco and the lingering memory of its beauty, ours was a relationship flawed by an underlying cultural incompatibility. We were never meant for marriage" (Anderson 2000: 105).

The reflexive approach, as we have just seen, can enhance the fieldwork experience. It can give depth to the data collection and provide greater insights. It can result in a richer and more nuanced view of the culture under study. However, if taken to extreme, only focusing on our own experiences can blind us to what we are there

to observe. A word of caution, then, about the reflexive approach
from Beyer:

> At its best, such postmodernist fieldwork promotes self-critical
> awareness, sensitivity to presuppositions, and continuous dia-
> logue between the interpreter and interpreted. But it can also
> produce obsessively self-referential and self-congratulatory
> narratives, which assume that the fieldworker is much more
> interesting than the people being studied. (Beyer 2007)

Coming Home

WHEN DO WE LEAVE THE FIELD?

In years past, it took months to reach the field site. And once home again, the site was far away. Today, when anthropologists return home, they are still connected to their field site—email, Facebook, Skype, and cell phones are just some of the technologies that keep us close. And with most anthropologists doing fieldwork at home, the field site is only a short trip across town. Data continues to be readily available, but obligations also continue. At home or far away, there is the expectation on the part of your community that the anthropologist will maintain the same close relationships. So when does the field end? Today it seems it never does. And today, also, the field can come to you. "A barefoot village kid who used to trail along after you *will* one day show up on your doorstep with an Oxford degree and your book in hand" (Wolf 1992: 137).

AND HOW DO WE COPE?

I am standing at an intersection waiting for the traffic light to change so I can cross the street. I wait and wait and wait. It isn't until I begin to look around that I notice a pole with a large button: Ah, press the button, the light changes. We have returned to Los Angeles, to the same apartment we left three years before. I had crossed this street, and pressed that button, hundreds of times, without thinking about it. Now, everything seems foreign and I don't know how to do the simplest things. This is part of what we call culture shock—what was familiar is now unfamiliar and, just as you had to integrate yourself in the field, now you are reintegrating yourself into your own culture. And it is not easy. Whereas my small children were welcome everywhere in Mexico, here I find myself ostracized as a mother: Higher-end restaurants and some not so high-end, theaters, movie houses, and fancy stores are all "closed" to me if I have a toddler in a stroller. Whereas in Mexico children were brought to late-night parties where they played, then slept on the coats strewn on beds until collected by their parents, here they were not included in the invitation. I found myself bursting into tears for no reason. When we became particularly homesick for Mexico, we would drive to a Spanish-speaking part of town with its bakeries, restaurants, stores, and people who felt more familiar to us. I cannot give you a formula for overcoming culture shock, but knowing about it will make you feel less alone, and knowing that it will pass is also reassuring.

References

Abu-Lughod, Lila. 1997. "The Interpretation of Culture(s) After Television." *Representations* 59 (Summer): 109–134.

Acheson, James M. 1988. *The Lobster Gangs of Maine*. Hanover, NH: University Press of New England.

American Anthropological Association. "Anthropology: Education for the 21st Century." Retrieved from http://www.americananthro.org/ AdvanceYourCareer/Content.aspx?ItemNumber=1782

American Friends Service Committee. (2014). "Letter to Clarence Pickett Regarding Japanese Internment-1942." Retrieved from http://afsc.org/ sites/afsc.civicactions.net/files/documents/Letter%20about% 20mistreatment%20of%20Japanese-Americans.pdf

American Red Cross. 2007, May. *Congressional Charter of the American National Red Cross*. Retrieved from http://www.redcross.org/images/ MEDIA_CustomProductCatalog/m4240124_charter.pdf

Anderson, Barbara Gallatin. 2000. *Around the World in 30 Years: Life as a Cultural Anthropologist*. Long Grove, IL: Waveland Press.

Anderson, Benedict. 1983. *Imagined Communities: Reflections on the Origin and Spread of Nationalism*. London: Verso.

Angrosino, Michael V. 2007. *Naturalistic Observation*. Book 1 of *Qualitative Essentials*. Walnut Creek, CA: Left Coast Press.

Arita, Akiko. 1994. "Photographic Study of Contemporary Navajo Culture: Reflecting the Native View." MA thesis, California State University, Northridge.

Asmi, Rehenuma. 2011. "Fieldwork and Motherwork in the Middle East," *Anthropology News* 52 (5): 33.

Baca Zinn, Maxine. 2001. "Insider Field Research in Minority Communities." In *Contemporary Field Research: Perspectives and Formulations*, 2nd ed., edited by Robert M. Emerson, pp. 159–166. Long Grove, IL: Waveland Press.

Barley, Nigel. 2000 [1983]. *The Innocent Anthropologist: Notes from a Mud Hut*. Long Grove, IL: Waveland Press. (Originally published London: Penguin Books, 1983.)

Bateson, Gregory, and Margaret Mead. (1942, December). *Balinese Character: A Photographic Analysis*, vol. II, edited by Wilbur G. Valentine. New York: Special Publications of the New York Academy of Sciences.

Bateson, Mary Catherine. 2001. "Words for a New Century." In *Growing up in New Guinea: A Comparative Study of Primitive Education*, by Margaret Mead, pp. xi–xiv. New York: Perennial Classics.

Baxandall, Michael. (1991). "Exhibiting Intention: Some Preconditions of the Visual Display of Culturally Purposeful Objects." In *Exhibiting Cultures: The Poetics and Politics of Museum Display,* edited by Ivan Karp and Steven D. Lavine, pp. 33–41. Washington, DC: Smithsonian Institute Press.

Bernard, H. Russell. 2011. *Research Methods in Anthropology: Qualitative and Quantitative Approaches,* 5th ed. Lanham, MD: Altamira Press.

Bernard, H. Russell, and Clarence C. Gravlee, eds. 2015. *Handbook of Methods in Cultural Anthropology*, 2nd ed. Lanham, Maryland: Rowman and Littlefield.

Beyer, Steve. 2007, December 4. "Extraordinary Anthropological Experiences." *Singing to the Plants, Steve Beyer's Blog on Ayahuasca and the Amazon*. Retrieved from http://www.singingtotheplants.com/2007/12/extraordinary-anthropological-experiences/

Bird, S. Elizabeth, and Jessica Barber. 2007. "Constructing a Virtual Ethnography." In *Doing Cultural Anthropology: Projects for Ethnographic Data Collection*, 2nd ed., edited by Michael V. Angrosino, pp. 139–148. Long Grove, IL: Waveland Press.

Boas, Franz. 1928. *Anthropology and Modern Life*. New York: W.W. Norton.

Boellstorff, Tom. 2008. *Coming of Age in Second Life: An Anthropologist Explores the Virtually Human*. Princeton: Princeton University Press.

———. 2009. "Virtual Worlds and Futures of Anthropology." *Anthronotes* 30 (1) (Spring): 1–5.

Bowen, Elenore Smith. 1964. *Return to Laughter: An Anthropological Novel*. New York: Doubleday.

Brettell, Caroline. 2000. "Fieldwork in the Archives: Methods and Sources in Historical Anthropology." In *Handbook of Methods in Cultural Anthropology*, edited by H. Russell Bernard, pp. 513–546. Lanham, MD: Altamira Press.

Briggs, Charles L. 1984. "Learning How to Ask: Native Metacommunicative Competence and the Incompetence of Fieldworkers." *Language and Society* 13: 1–28.

Browne, Katherine E. 2015. *Standing in the Need: Culture, Comfort, and Coming Home After Katrina*. Austin: University of Texas Press.

Camp Harmony News-Letters. 1997 [1942]. University Libraries, University of Washington. Retrieved from https://www.lib.washington.edu/exhibits/harmony/Newsletter/

Clifford, James. 1990. "Notes on (Field)Notes." In *Fieldnotes: The Making of Anthropology,* edited by Roger Sanjek, pp. 47–70. Ithaca, NY: Cornell University Press.

———. 1991. "Four Northwest Coast Museums: Travel Reflections." In *Exhibiting Cultures: The Poetics and Politics of Museum Display*, edited by Ivan Karp and Steven D. Lavine, pp. 213–254. Washington, DC: Smithsonian Institute Press.

———. 1997. *Routes: Travel and Translation in the Late Twentieth Century*. Cambridge, MA: Harvard University Press.

Collier, John, Jr. 1988. "Visual Anthropology and the Future of Ethnographic Film." In *Anthropological Filmmaking*, edited by J. R. Rollwagen, pp. 73–96. New York: Harwood Academic Press.

Conrad, Joseph. 1942, April. "Japanese Evacuation Report No. 8." Joseph Conrad, Collector, Box 3, Notebook. Hoover Institution Archives.

David, Alexandra. 2009. "Risky business: Aspiring Hollywood Actors and the Selling of the Self." PhD Dissertation. UCLA.

DeWalt, Kathleen, and Billie R. DeWalt. 2011. *Participant Observation: A Guide for Fieldworkers*, 2nd ed. Lanham MD: Altamira Press.

DeWalt, Kathleen, and Billie R. DeWalt, with Coral B. Wayland. 2000. "Participant Observation." In *Handbook of Methods in Cultural Anthropology*, edited by H. Russell Bernard, pp. 259–299. Lanham, MD: Altamira Press.

Doud, Richard. 1964, May 22. Oral history interview with Dorothea Lange 1964 May 22. Smithsonian Archives of American Art, Smithsonian Institution. Retrieved from http://www.aaa.si.edu/collections/interviews/oral-history-interview-dorothea-lange-11757.

Doyle, Sir Arthur Conan. 2010 [1892]. *The Adventures of Sherlock Holmes*. New York: Harper Collins. (Originally published London: George Newnes, Ltd., 1892.)

Drew, Georgina. 2009. "Whose Representation? Power and Voice in a Photojournalism Project." *Anthropology News* (April): 8–9.

Dubisch, Jill. 1995. "Lovers in the Field: Sex, Dominance and the Female Anthropologist." In *Taboo: Sex, Identity and Erotic Subjectivity in Anthropological Fieldwork*, edited by Don Kulick and Margaret Willson, pp. 22–28. New York: Routledge.

Durrenberger, Paul, and Karaleah S. Reichart. 2012. *The Anthropology of Labor Unions*. Boulder, CO: University Press of Colorado.

El Guindi, Fadwa. 2000. "From Pictorializing to Visual Anthropology." In *Handbook of Methods in Cultural Anthropology*, edited by. H. Russell Bernard, pp. 459–511. Lanham, MD: Altamira Press.

Emerson, Robert M. 2001. *Contemporary Field Research: Perspectives and Formulations,* 2nd ed. Long Grove, IL: Waveland Press.

Emerson, Robert M., Rachel I. Fretz, and Linda L. Shaw. (2011). *Writing Ethnographic Fieldnotes*, 2nd ed. Chicago: University of Chicago Press

Evans-Pritchard, E. E. 1937. *Witchcraft, Oracles and Magic among the Azande*. Oxford: Clarendon Press.

Fish, Adam. 2011. "The Place of the Internet in Anthropology." *Anthropology News* 52 (3): 17.

Fox, Kate. *The Smell Report*. Social Issues Research Center. n.d. Retrieved from http://www.sirc.org/publik/smell_human.html

Friedl, Ernestine. 1991. "Colleague and Friend: A Reminiscence of Hortense Powdermaker." *Journal of Anthropological Research* 47 (4): 473–478.

Gallagher, Edward J. n.d. "The *Enola Gay* Controversy," *History on Trial*, Lehigh University Digital Library. Retrieved from http://digital.lib.lehigh.edu/trial/index.html

Geertz, Clifford. 1973. *The Interpretation of Cultures: Selected Essays*. New York: Basic Books.

Gershon, Ilana. 2012. *The Breakup 2.0: Disconnecting over New Media*. Ithaca, NY: Cornell University Press.

Goffman, Erving. 2001. "On Fieldwork." In *Contemporary Field Research: Per-spectives and Formulations*, 2nd ed., edited by Robert M. Emerson, pp. 153–158. Long Grove, IL: Waveland Press.

Greenhouse, Carol J. 1985. "Anthropology at Home: Whose Home?" *Human Organization* 44 (3): 261–264.

Grimes, Kimberly M., and B. Lynne Milgram, eds. 2000. *Artisans and Cooper-atives: Developing Alternative Trade for the Global Economy*. Tucson: University of Arizona Press.

Grunenfelder, Julia. 2014. "A Foreign Woman Researcher in a Purdah Soci-ety: Opportunities and Challenges for Knowledge Production in the 2000s." *Human Organization* 73(3): 214–223.

Halperin, Rhoda. 1998. *Practicing Community: Class Culture and Power in an Urban Neighborhood*. Austin: University of Texas Press.

Halpern, Matthew. 2013. "The Digital Gamer: An Anthropological Investiga-tion of On-Line Gaming Communities." MA thesis, California State Uni-versity, Northridge.

Hamabata, Matthews Masayuki. 1991. *Crested Kimono: Power and Love in the Japanese Business Family*. Ithaca, New York: Cornell University Press.

Harlow, Nora, ed. 1983. *Special Street: History of the 1500 Block of Altivo Way, Los Angeles, California. Elysian Heights. Part 1*. Los Angeles: Echo Park Historical Park Archives.

Harris, Marvin. 1987. *Why Nothing Works: The Anthropology of Daily Life*, rev. ed. New York: Touchstone Book.

Hayano, David. 1982. *Poker Faces: The Life and Work of Professional Card Players*. Oakland: University of California Press.

Hong, Lawrence K., and Robert W. Duff. 2002. "Modulated Participant-Obser-vation: Managing the Dilemma of Distance in Field Research." *Field Methods* 14 (2): 190–196

Jackson, Jean E. (1990a). "'Deja Entendu': The Liminal Qualities of Anthropo-logical Fieldnotes." *Journal of Contemporary Ethnography* 13 (1): 8–43.

———. (1990b). "I am a Fieldnote: Fieldnotes as a Symbol of Professional Identity." In *Fieldnotes: The Makings of Anthropology*, edited by Roger Sanjek, pp. 3–33. Ithaca, NY: Cornell University Press.

———. 2016. "Changes in Fieldnotes Practice Over the Past Thirty Years in US Anthropology." In *eFieldnotes: The Makings of Anthropology in the Digital World*, edited by Roger Sanjek and Susan W. Tratner, pp. 42–62. Philadelphia: University of Pennsylvania Press.

Kehoe, Alice. 2003. "Potlatch." *Encyclopedia of Food and Culture*. *Encyclopedia.com*. Retrieved from http://www.encyclopedia.com/doc/1G2-3403400490.html

Kishlansky, Mark A. 2003. *Sources of World History, Volume 1*, 3rd ed. New York: Longman Publishers, 2003.

Kishlansky, Mark A., et al. 1991. "How to Read a Document." In *Sources of the West: Readings for Western Civilization, Volume 1: From the Beginning to 1648*, edited by Mark A. Kishlansky and Victor Louis, pp. xi–xix. New York: HarperCollins.

Kuehling, Susanne. 2009. "Capturing Scent through Image: Oceanic Experi-ences of Family and Home." *Anthropology News* 50 (4): 14.

Kulick, Don, and Margaret Willson, eds. 1995. *Taboo: Sex, Identity and Erotic Subjectivity in Anthropological Fieldwork*. New York: Routledge.

Le Guin, Ursula K. 2004. *The Wave in the Mind: Talks and Essays on the Writer, the Reader, and the Imagination*. Boston: Shambala Publications.

Leitner, Helga. 2012. "Spaces of Encounters: Immigration, Race, Class, and the Politics of Belonging in Small-Town America." *Annals of the Association of American Geographers* 102 (4): 828–846.

Lutkehaus, Nancy. 1990. "Refractions of Reality: On the Use of Other Ethnographers' Fieldnotes." In *Fieldnotes: The Making of Anthropology*, edited by Roger Sanjek, pp. 303–323. Ithaca: NY: Cornell University Press.

Malinowski, Bronislaw. 1928. *The Sexual Life of Savages in North-Western Melanesia: An Ethnographic Account of Courtship, Marriage and Family Life among the Natives of the Trobriand Islands British New Guinea*. New York: Harcourt Brace and World.

———. 2013 [1922]. *Argonauts of the Western Pacific: An Account of Native Enterprise and Adventure in the Archipelagoes of Melanesian New Guinea,* enhanced ed. Long Grove, IL: Waveland Press. (Originally published New York: E. P. Dutton & Company, 1922.)

Markowitz, Fran, and Michael Ashkenazi. 1999 *Sex, Sexuality and the Anthropologist*. Chicago: University of Illinois Press.

Marti, F. Alethea. 2013. Classroom Material.

Marti, Judith. 1990. "Subsistence and the State: Municipal Government Policies and Urban Markets in Developing Nations, The Case of Mexico City and Guadalajara, 1877–1910." PhD dissertation, University of California, Los Angeles.

———. 1994. "Vendors and the Government: A Case Study in Institutional Economics." In *Anthropology and Institutional Economics: Monographs in Economic Anthropology, No. 12*, edited by James M. Acheson, pp. 195–211. New York: University Press of America.

———. 2001. "Nineteenth-Century Views of Women's Participation in Mexico's Markets. In *Women Traders in Cross-Cultural Perspective: Mediating Identity, Marketing Wares*, edited by Linda J. Seligman, pp. 16–44. Stanford, CA: Stanford University Press.

Mead, Margaret. 1928. *Coming of Age in Samoa: A Psychological Study of Primitive Youth for Western Civilization*. New York: William Morrow and Co.

———. 1962 [1942]. *And Keep Your Powder Dry: An Anthropologist Looks at America*. New York: HarperCollins, Perennial Classics Edition.

———. 1993. "Samoa: The Adolescent Girl." In *The Other Fifty Percent: Multicultural Perspective on Gender Relations*, edited by Mari Womack and Judith Marti, pp. 69–83. Long Grove, IL: Waveland Press.

Mendoza-Denton, Norma. 2008. *Homegirls: Language and Cultural Practice among Latina Youth Gangs*. Malden, MA: Blackwell.

Miller, Laura. 2012, September 13. "I Don't Think I Like My Fieldwork Site." *Savage Minds*. Retrieved from http://savageminds.org/author/lauramiller/

Muller-Wille, Ludger, ed. 1998. *Franz Boas among the Inuit of Baffin Island, 1883–1884, Journals and Letters*. Translated by William Barr. Toronto: University of Toronto Press.

Musante (DeWalt), Kathleen. 2015. "Participant Observation." In *Handbook of Methods in Cultural Anthropology,* 2nd ed., edited by Russell H. Bernard and Clarence C. Gravlee, pp. 251–292. Lanham, MD: Rowman and Littlefield.

Nardi, Bonnie A. 2010. *My Life as a Night Elf Priest: An Anthropological Account of World of Warcraft.* Ann Arbor: University of Michigan Press.

Nash, June, and Helen Safa, eds. 1986. *Women and Change in Latin America.* South Hadley, MA: Bergin & Garvey Publishers.

Newon, Lisa. 2011. "Multimodal Creativity and Identities of Expertise in the Digital Ecology of a World of Warcraft Guild." In *Digital Discourse: Language in the New Media*, edited by Crispin Thurlow and Kristine Mroczek, pp. 131–153. New York: Oxford University Press.

Ochs, Elinor, and Tamar Kremer-Sadlik, eds. 2013. *Fast Forward Family: Home, Work and Relationships in Middle-Class America.* Berkeley: University of California Press.

Olin, Chuck. 1983. *Box of Treasures.* (Transcript of film). Edited by Razan Alzayani. Documentary Educational Resources. Retrieved from http://der.org/resources/study-guides/box-of-treasures-study-guide.pdf

"Online Document: North Dakota is Absorbing Kurdish Refugees." 1996, December 9. *Minneapolis-St. Paul Star Tribune.* Retrieved from http://www.deseretnews.com/article/529884/ONLINE-DOCUMENT--NORTH-DAKOTA-IS-ABSORBING-KURDISH-REFUGEES

Ortner, Sherry. 2010. "Access: Reflections on Studying Up in Hollywood." *Ethnography* 11(2): 211–233.

Petersen, Glenn. 2012, May 25. "How to Be an Anthropologist." *The Chronicle of Higher Education*, p. B20.

Plattner, Stuart. 1998. *High Art Down Home: An Economic Ethnography of a Local Art Market.* Chicago: University of Chicago Press.

Pollard, Amy. 2009. "Field of Screams: Difficulty and Ethnographic Fieldwork." *Anthropology Matters, North America* 11(2). Retrieved from http://www.anthropologymatters.com/index.php?journal=anth_matters&page=article&op=view&path%5B%5D=10&path%5B%5D=10

Powdermaker, Hortense. 1933. *Life in Lesu: The Study of a Melanesian Society in New Ireland.* Norton, MA: Norton Library.

———. 1939. *After Freedom: A Cultural Study in the Deep South.* New York: Viking Press.

———. 1950. *Hollywood, The Dream Factory: An Anthropologist Studies the Movie Makers.* Boston: Little, Brown.

———. 1966. *Stranger and Friend: The Way of Anthropologists.* New York: W. W. Norton & Company.

———. 1993. "A Woman Alone in the Field." In *The Other Fifty Percent: Multicultural Perspective on Gender Relations*, edited by Mari Womack and Judith Marti, pp. 84–90. Long Grove, IL: Waveland Press.

Pulskamp, John R. 2006. "Proletarianization of Professional Work and Changed Workplace Relationships." In *Labor in Cross Cultural Perspective*, edited by E. Paul Durrenberger and Judith E. Marti, pp. 175–192. Lanham, MD: Altamira Press.

Read, Kenneth E. 1965. *The High Valley.* New York: Charles Schribner's Sons.

Redfield, Robert. 1930. *Tepoztlan: A Mexican Village-A Study of Folk Life.* Chicago: University of Chicago Press, 1930.

Rees, Martha Woodson. 2013. "Ayuda or Work?: Labor History of Female Heads of Household from Oaxaca." In *Labor in Cross Cultural Perspective*, edited by E. Paul Durrenberger and Judith E. Marti, pp. 87–109. Lanham, MD: Altamira Press.

"Report of the American Red Cross Survey of Assembly Centers in California, Oregon, and Washington." 1984 [1942, August]. In *Papers of the U.S. Commission on Wartime Relocation and Internment of Civilians. Part 1*, edited by Randolph Boehm, Numerical file archive, p. 15, Reel 10, Box 11. Frederick, MD: University Publications of America. Retrieved from http://www.lib.washington.edu/exhibits/harmony/Newsletter/

Richards-Greaves, Gillian. 2013. "Going Home: The Native Ethnographer's Baggage and the Crisis of Representation." *Anthropology News* 54 (8): 15–16.

Rosaldo, Renato. 1993. *Culture and Truth: the Remaking of Social Analysis.* Boston: Beacon Press.

Sanjek, Roger, ed. 1990a. *Fieldnotes: The Makings of Anthropology*. Ithaca, New York: Cornell University Press.

———. 1990b. "A Vocabulary for Fieldnotes." In *Fieldnotes: The Making of Anthropology*, edited by Roger Sanjek, pp. 92–138. Ithaca NY: Cornell University Press.

Siemens, Stephen David. (1993). "Access to Women's Knowledge: The Azande Experience." In *The Other Fifty Percent: Multicultural Perspective on Gender Relations*, edited by Mari Womack and Judith Marti, pp. 91–98. Long Grove, IL: Waveland Press.

Singer, Natasha. (2014, February 14). "Intel's Sharp-Eyed Social Scientist." *New York Times*. Retrieved from http://www.nytimes.com/2014/02/16/technology/intels-sharp-eyed-social-scientist.html?_r=0

Smith, Paul Chaat, and Herbert R. Rosen. (2011, January 5). "Narration: This is about History and the Past—Two Different Things." Display text. Washington, DC: National Museum of the American Indian, Smithsonian Institution.

Spradley, James. 2016 [1979]. *The Ethnographic Interview*. Long Grove, IL: Waveland Press. (Originally published Belmont CA: Wadsworth Cengage Learning, 1979.)

———. *Participant Observation*. 2016 [1980]. Long Grove, IL: Waveland Press. (Originally published New York: Holt, Rinehart and Winston. 1980.)

Stocking, George W. Jr. 1983. "The Ethnographer's Magic: Fieldwork in British Anthropology from Tylor to Malinowski." In *Observers Observed: Essays on Ethnographic Fieldwork*, edited by George W. Stocking, Jr., 70–120. History of Anthropology Series, vol. 1. Madison: University of Wisconsin Press.

Tierney, Gerry. (2007). "Becoming a Participant Observer." In *Doing Cultural Anthropology: Projects in Ethnographic Data Collection*, 2nd ed., edited by Michael V. Angrosino, pp. 9–18. Long Grove, IL: Waveland Press.

U'Mista Cultural Society. n.d. "History." Retrieved from http://www.umista.ca/about/history.php

Wilkins, David P. 1992. "Linguistic Research under Aboriginal Control: A Personal Account of Fieldwork in Central Australia." *Australian Journal of Linguistics* 12:171–200.

Williams, Bianca C. 2011. "What I Now Know about Completing Fieldwork." *Anthropology News* 52 (5): 28.

Willson, Margaret. 1995. "Afterword Perspective and Difference: Sexualization, the Field, and the Ethnographer." In *Taboo: Sex, Identity and Erotic Subjectivity in Anthropological Fieldwork*, edited by Don Kulick and Margaret Willson, pp. 190–207. New York: Routledge.

Wilson, Samuel M., and Leighton C. Peterson. 2002. "The Anthropology of Online Communities." *Annual Review of Anthropology* 31 (October): 449–467.

Wolf, Margery. 1992. *A Thrice-Told Tale: Feminism, Postmodernism, and Ethnographic Responsibility*. Stanford, CA: Stanford University Press.

Ypeij, Annelou. 1998 "'KABOOM . . . Yet another Bomb, Reflections on Fieldwork and a Text.'" In *Anthropology of Difference: Essays in Honour of Professor Arie de Ruijter*, edited by Els van Dongen and Selma van Londen, pp. 85–97. Utrecht, Netherlands: ISOR.

Zeitlyn, David. 2003. "Don't Cut There But There." *Anthropology News* 44 (6): 68.

Index